Disaster
Recovery Planning

Steven M. Bragg

AccountingTools®

ISBN 978-1-64221-163-4

For more information about AccountingTools® products, visit our Web site at www.accountingtools.com.

Table of Contents

About the Author

Steven Bragg, CPA, has been the chief financial officer or controller of four companies, as well as a consulting manager at Ernst & Young. He received a master's degree in finance from Bentley College, an MBA from Babson College, and a Bachelor's degree in Economics from the University of Maine. He has been a two-time president of the Colorado Mountain Club, and is an avid alpine skier, mountain biker, and certified master diver. Mr. Bragg resides in Centennial, Colorado. He has written more than 300 books and courses, including *New Controller Guidebook*, *GAAP Guidebook*, and *Payroll Management*.

Steven maintains the accountingtools.com web site, which contains continuing professional education courses, the Accounting Best Practices podcast, and thousands of articles on accounting subjects.

Buy Additional AccountingTools Courses

AccountingTools offers more than 1,500 hours of CPE courses, with concentrations in accounting, auditing, finance, taxation, and ethics. Related courses that you might like include:

- Business Insurance Fundamentals
- Enterprise Risk Management

Go to accountingtools.com/cpe to view these additional courses.

AccountingTools®

Chapter 1
Project Planning Considerations

Introduction

The typical manager must deal with a variety of issues in order to run a business, including the development of new products, deciding how to sell them, arranging for appropriate financing, and creating an organization to support it. What typically falls through the cracks is how to deal with a range of possible disasters, any of which could take down the company. For example, a key supplier facility might be located in a flood plain, or unusually dry conditions could cause the local power company to shut off its power delivery as a protective measure, in order to keep sparks from triggering forest fires. Or, a regime change in another country could put a company facility at risk of expropriation by a new and hostile government. And as we have now learned, a pandemic can shut down an entire business sector overnight. Any executive needs to be aware of these possibilities, and develop plans to both protect company assets and maintain operations in the face of a range of possible disasters.

In this book, we discuss how to create a disaster recovery plan, which is intended not only to minimize the damage caused by destructive events, but also to assist in a firm's recovery efforts. When this plan is well-designed and updated regularly to deal with the latest events, it can be a major corporate asset.

The Disaster Recovery Planning Process

The development of a proper disaster recovery plan is not a scattershot endeavor. Instead, it calls for a detailed, formal planning process. In-depth planning is needed to ensure that all relevant parties are involved in the planning process.

Planning is usually triggered by an event that wakes up management in regard to the dangers faced by the business. For example, it might experience a disaster directly, or see what happens when a disaster hits a competitor. It is also possible that the firm's outside auditors will recommend that a disaster recovery plan be developed as part of its annual letter to management. If senior management is convinced of the need for a plan, then one or more of them becomes the project sponsor, who is responsible for driving the process forward.

> **Note:** If senior management has decided to create a disaster recovery plan only because the outside auditors have recommended doing so, it is more likely that only a minimal plan will be created, just to say that the requirement has been met.

The project sponsor should be someone with enough authority within the organization to give the planning project a high degree of credibility and support. The sponsor should also be in a position to obtain adequate resources for the project. An additional (and essential) role for the sponsor is being able to force the various department heads to cooperate with the project as it progresses; to accomplish this, the sponsor needs to be positioned higher in the organizational hierarchy than any of the department managers.

> **Tip:** If the sponsor's interest in the disaster recovery plan fades, then so too will the project. Consequently, it makes sense to ascertain any prospective sponsor's reasons for supporting the project.

The sponsor's main initial task is to assign someone to take on the role of project manager (PM). The ideal PM is able to work with a broad array of people, because the disaster recovery plan encompasses every nook and cranny of a business. In this role, the PM must be strongly supported by the sponsor, because it is quite likely that multiple parties within the firm will not see the need for the plan, and so will try to give it a low priority – if not kill it off entirely.

The sponsor and PM jointly define the scope of the project, its timeline, and the expected project outcome. A key part of these decisions is setting them to match the amount of corporate resources (both in terms of staff and funding) that will be made available to the project.

Based on the initial decisions made, the project manager then brings together a team that develops a detailed plan and conducts initial testing to ensure that it functions as expected. The plan is likely to be extensive, including multiple levels of tasks to be completed, along with sequencing to ensure that preliminary tasks are completed before follow-on activities are begun.

It is generally better to assemble a relatively small group of team members, from which a larger group may be added over a period of time, depending on how the project progresses. Since these people are being taken away from their regular jobs within the company, it is essential to only assign them to the team when they are really needed, and then to release them back to their regular jobs as soon as possible. Members of the team may eventually include some or all of the positions described in the following exhibit.

Disaster Recovery Planning Project Team Members

Position Name	Assigned Planning Areas
Facilities manager	Environmental controls, fire suppression, flood mitigation, structural issues, and utilities
Legal counsel	The legal ramifications of planned actions
Line managers	Prioritization of failure issues within their areas of responsibility
Public relations	Prepared contact lists with the surrounding community, based on the nature of the disaster
Purchasing staff	Communications with suppliers
Sales staff	Communications with customers
Security manager	Evacuations, limitations on facility access, and theft prevention

Anyone assigned to the team as a department liaison should have a firm knowledge of how their department operates, its major process flows, and its systems. With such knowledge, a liaison can minimize any additional research into how his or her department operates. Another beneficial knowledge item is having dealt with disasters in their department before – this gives them an enhanced knowledge of the weak points in their department's processes. This usually means that someone with a relatively high experience level should be assigned to the team. When an assigned liaison turns out to not have the requisite level of expertise, the PM should have the project sponsor intervene, to obtain a more appropriate liaison.

Tip: In order to be most effective in utilizing the time of department liaisons, schedule them to join the team one at a time, in sequence. By doing so, the core team members can concentrate on disaster planning for one department at a time, after which the liaison can be released from working with the team.

Each element of the plan should be based on a standard template. Doing so ensures that the same layout and information content can be found in each aspect of the plan, so that the overall plan appears more coherent to users. In addition, the use of a template makes it easier for team members to write their portions of the plan, since the structure of the template prompts them for the types of information to write.

Tip: Provide standard training to team members in plan writing. Doing so makes them more efficient in how they tackle the work, and also increases the likelihood that the team's writing will encompass the same general topics and address the same issues. In short, training results in more consistent writing.

As the project unfolds, the PM is responsible for monitoring the progress of all tasks, and stepping in to assign additional resources where tasks are falling behind their scheduled due dates. In addition, the PM keeps all key project stakeholders appraised of progress, as well as any issues encountered that may delay project completion or require additional resources.

Project stakeholders include anyone who has an interest in the project. The types of information to send to these people depends in large part on their motivations. For example, the manager of the production department whose equipment failure just caused the company to incur a $1 million loss in the last quarter is highly motivated to have a recovery plan completed for that same equipment. In such cases of extreme interest, the PM may need to communicate information directly to a stakeholder. In other cases, a monthly summary of work performed may be sufficient. Thus, a tailored approach to keeping stakeholders informed may be necessary. However, this tailored approach should be developed from a cost-benefit perspective, since it can become excessively burdensome for the PM to engage in a different reporting mechanism with each individual stakeholder.

> **Tip:** Develop a matrix that details the nature and timing of the communications to be made with each stakeholder.

The PM may decide to hire outside consultants to assist with the development of the plan. This is an excellent idea for the more technical aspects of the plan, especially those pertaining to information technology, where a consultant might be able to provide guidance in areas where the project team lacks expertise. While the associated consulting fees may be substantial, the level of expertise provided should more than offset them. In particular, a knowledgeable consultant can keep the process on track, so that it is completed on time – which keeps the project from incurring additional costs. However, consultants should not run the project; they do not have a detailed understanding of how the company operates, and so they are better placed with the team as advisors, not managers.

> **Tip:** A good reason not to have a consultant be the PM is that the consultant will move on after the project has been completed – leaving no in-house champion to continue supporting it.

Once the disaster recovery plan has been completed, the PM ensures that all aspects of it have been thoroughly documented, and then hands off the plan to whoever has been assigned the task of maintaining it. The party taking over the plan is likely to actually be several people, since at least one person in each major department will need to be involved.

Ongoing administration of the plan is not a minor affair. It involves revising the plan in conjunction with the rollout of new products, processes, and company locations, since each of these events may mitigate some risks or add others. In addition, the plan administration team must schedule ongoing tests of the plan within each department on a rolling basis, so that it is being evaluated at regular intervals. Each of these tests will likely find some issues that will call for revisions to the plan. The plan may also be tested for specific threats, such as flood damage or the loss of power, to see how well it performs. The need for these ongoing activities means that disaster recovery planning should be an integral part of the planning processes of a business.

Project Scope

The scope of the project to develop a disaster recovery plan is critical to how comprehensive it turns out to be, as well as its odds of success. When the scope is set to encompass an entire business, it can be challenging to complete the work, because it calls for the cooperation of every single department in the organization – which can be difficult to obtain. In this situation, the odds of project failure increase dramatically. Conversely, if the scope of the project is limited to just a small area, such as one department, then it has excellent odds of success, since the cooperation of only a small group of people is needed. However, when the scope is so small, the project's impact on the organization is correspondingly reduced. Given the issues associated with these positions at either end of the continuum for project scope, it can be a delicate matter to set the project at just the right amount to achieve a successful project that still has a meaningful impact on the organization. A reasonable outcome that many organizations pursue is a measured rollout of the project scope, so that the project gradually encompasses more company operations over time, building on the success (and experience) achieved through the early phases of the project.

EXAMPLE

The Farthingale Printing Company operates a large, multi-million-dollar automated printing press, along with a variety of lesser machines for smaller printing jobs. Other key departments cover print design work and sales. The company has never created a disaster recovery plan, and there is some resistance to it from the department heads. Because of these issues, the company president decides to initially develop a plan just for the automated printing press, in order to have alternatives available if the press is damaged or destroyed.

EXAMPLE

The Multi-Line Company, as its name implies, sells a broad range of products, none of which comprise more than 5% of its total sales. All operations are conducted from a single building complex. Since there is no single area on which to focus a disaster recovery plan, management decides to begin with a plan that focuses solely on maintaining the flow of electricity into the company. This focus benefits every part of the firm, since a loss of power would halt all company operations to an equal extent.

An example of the statement of scope associated with the second of the preceding examples is as follows:

> Write an emergency contingency plan to address the possibility of a loss of electrical power to all parts of the company. Include recommendations for the acquisition of emergency power backup facilities, as well as related procedures, decision trees, and employee training.

Additional considerations for the preceding scope statement are determining which functions to shut down while the company is operating under emergency power, such as air conditioning systems. The scope might also address related utilities, such as the provision of gas, water, and telecommunications capabilities to the company.

Tip: If the plan is being developed as the result of an auditor recommendation or Board mandate, then the date by which a plan must be presented to either party drives its scope. Thus, if a plan is required by the next quarterly board meeting, then the scope must be narrow in order to ensure that the plan will be completed on time.

Ideally, the project scope should only encompass a process whose failure would have a material impact on the business. For example, the destruction of the janitorial department by a tornado will probably not have much of an impact on company revenues, since it can be readily outsourced. However, the outright failure of the bottleneck operation on the manufacturing floor could bring a company to its knees, and so requires a recovery plan.

Another way to view the level of scope to be assigned is the extent to which the company is willing to maintain the plan. A highly detailed and comprehensive plan may call for significant ongoing staffing to keep it operational, while a tightly-focused plan will require a correspondingly smaller amount of time to oversee.

Project Duration

The duration of a plan to develop a disaster recovery plan will vary, depending on its scope. Nonetheless, it is reasonable to expect a typical project to last for about six months. Of this time period, roughly two-thirds is devoted to the project set-up, training, and plan development phases, while the remaining one-third is needed to test and revise the plan.

When the duration of a project extends beyond six months, the likelihood of project failure increases, because management attention is more likely to be drawn to other priorities, resulting in a loss of management support. Consequently, when the duration will probably be more than six months, consider shaving the project scope down to a more manageable level, where it can be completed within a more reasonable timeframe.

Planning Minimum Requirements

When developing a disaster recovery plan, it can be useful to set lower boundaries for what it shall include. At a minimum, it should address every process and piece of equipment within the company that is judged to be critical to the finances and operations of the business. This may result in what appears to be a scattershot plan, as it could touch upon a broad range of highly-targeted areas within the company, but has the benefit of protecting the firm from its most critical risks.

Another minimum requirement is that the plan be understandable to anyone assigned to implement it. Recovery plans tend to be written by experts with an in-depth knowledge of the subject matter, while those implementing assigned tasks have significantly less expertise. Consequently, the plan must be reviewed and tested by someone other than the original author, and preferably by someone likely to be assigned to its implementation. The result may be significant changes in the text, to make procedures more understandable.

During the course of its work, the project team will likely find issues with the processes and equipment that fall within the scope of the project. The recovery plan should certainly be designed to mitigate these issues to the greatest extent possible. Nonetheless, another minimum requirement is to develop an issues list for delivery to senior management, with suggestions for how to fix them. Doing so can lead to significant process and equipment improvements, as well as declines in the associated risks.

Work Breakdown Structure

The initial construction of a plan for the team is to list the tasks that must be completed, estimating how long it will take to complete each one, assigning personnel to each task, and then developing a work sequence that positions these tasks in a logical flow. It can be useful to bring in a consultant for the development of this work breakdown structure, since they usually have access to standard lists of tasks for these types of plans, as well as for the estimated amount of time to complete each task.

Tip: Do not create a work breakdown structure in excessively fine-grained detail, since this creates a planning burden. Usually, any task expected to require less than one day can be incorporated into a related task.

It can be difficult to develop reasonable time estimates for project tasks. To enhance their accuracy, be sure to discuss the initial time expectation with the person assigned to each one, which may trigger a first round of changes to task durations. From this point forward, the PM should be willing to adjust the project scope or assign additional resources in order to complete each task by its assigned date; otherwise, there is an increased risk that downstream tasks will be negatively impacted by a prolonged task completion.

Once there is a reasonable idea of the time required for each task, the PM should estimate the total amount of labor needed to complete the project. This calculation may be used as the basis for an adjustment to the amount of staff resources assigned to the project – usually in an upward direction. At this point, the goal is to not only examine the total gap in resources available to the time required, but also the specific skill areas in which available resources fall short. The PM can use this information to request that specific parties be added to the team, and be able to request them for precisely-defined periods of time.

A particular concern when developing a work breakdown structure is to find the project bottleneck and figure out how to manage around it. For example, if the plan includes the IT department and the IT manager is the only person who can realistically formulate a disaster recovery plan for it, then this person could very well be the project bottleneck. The plan may need to be configured around the IT manager's availability. When developing a recovery plan, a common bottleneck is simply the number of people who can be assigned to the project. If the resource allocation will be on the low side, then a work breakdown structure will need to be devised that either restricts the project scope or extends the project duration – these being the only viable approaches to a resource constraint.

A refinement of the plan is to search for any cases in which team members are scheduled to work overtime on the project. This analysis should factor in the hours their regular bosses are still demanding of them, if they have been assigned to work part-time on the project. When planned overtime is present, the plan may need to be adjusted to stretch out completion dates or pare back project scope, so that overtime is minimized.

Planning Risk Areas

When developing the project plan, there are a number of planning risks to take into consideration. One concern is the presence of a completion date that has been mandated by senior management, usually to accede to a demand by the Board. When this is the case, the plan timeline may be so short that it is not realistic to develop a complete plan within the required period of time. Another concern is the aggregate and individual amount of experience assigned to the team. When experience levels are low (especially in regard to the PM), the project will probably take longer to complete. Yet another concern is the level of management support for the project. When the support level is low, the team will not be able to rely on consistent funding, and may also find that some of its members are pulled away to work on other tasks. An additional and relatively common risk is the impact of ongoing business interruptions on the work of the team. If there is any scheduled event (such as an off-site conference) that team members must attend, then the project will suffer. When these events are present, it can make sense to schedule project activities to begin after any expected interruptions. A final planning risk is the breadth of the company's functions that will be encompassed by the project. When there are many departments or locations involved, the complexity of the project increases, making it more difficult to manage. The PM should be aware of all these concerns, and examine them to see if any present a viable challenge to timely project completion.

Ongoing Planning Considerations

One of the most important planning considerations as a disaster recovery planning process proceeds is whether it is still on schedule for its pre-determined completion date. This information is needed not only to keep stakeholders informed, but also to maintain control over the amount of funds needed to complete the project, as well as the amount of staff time still required.

A good way to maintain proper oversight over the project is to load the expected task durations and dependencies into project planning software. By doing so, and then updating this information with actual task completion dates, the software will automatically generate revised milestone and project completion dates. This information can then be used to take a variety of actions, such as adding more resources to the project or cutting back on its scope – either of which are viable options when a project will run longer than expected.

At various points during a project, it is quite likely that suggestions will be made (or imposed) to expand the scope of the project. As a general rule, these suggestions should be vigorously opposed. The problem with scope expansion is that it increases the time required for project completion, and will probably call for the assignment of additional resources to the project – which may not be available. Consequently, when a scope expansion is made, a good comeback is to suggest that it be included in a subsequent phase of the project, rather than the current one.

Testing Schedule

Once the preliminary version of the plan has been completed, the next step is to test it. Testing is needed to spot any unaddressed areas in the plan, as well as to highlight any inconsistencies between different parts of it.

At its most basic level, testing involves a verbal walkthrough, where the PM and the responsible team member work their way through the written plan, discussing what is supposed to happen during each documented step. This testing iteration will likely uncover some needed adjustments. Once those adjustments have been made, the plan is examined by someone with knowledge of the targeted area, but who was not involved in the plan's development. Being an independent third party, this person is more likely to spot gaps and inconsistencies requiring correction. At this point, the plan can be tested for an entire department, after which the plan is evaluated and adjusted yet again. A final test is to simulate the disaster for which the plan was created (such as flooding), and evaluate how well the plan works when it is used as the basis for a recovery. This final step has the additional benefit of being a training tool, where those expected to actually use the plan are consulting it as part of their recovery efforts.

Once the disaster simulation has been completed, participants should meet with the team to develop a post mortem analysis of how well the plan worked. This analysis should focus on the strengths and weaknesses of the plan, noting specific areas in which improvements can be made. The notes from this meeting are then used to revise the plan further.

Project Termination

Once all of the preceding tasks have been completed, it is time to shut down the planning group and hand off the initial plan to a team that will administer it as an ongoing process. The new team will be managed by a plan administrator, who will ensure that the plan is regularly updated to accommodate changes in the business model. In addition, the administrator will be responsible for scheduling ongoing tests of the plan to ensure that it continues to address all targeted risk areas.

> **Tip:** The team could develop a boilerplate version of the disaster recovery plan, which can then be applied to each acquired business that the company subsequently purchases.

As part of the project shut down process, the PM should deliver a final accounting of where assigned funds were spent, as well as best practices uncovered and areas that fell short of expectations. Management can use this information whenever it decides to expand the scope of the firm's disaster recovery planning to additional areas of the business. Ideally, this report should allow for a better allocation of resources to similar projects in the future.

An essential element of the PM's final report should be a listing of all risk areas that the team uncovered, but which fell outside of the project scope. If possible, also note the extent of the planning effort that may be needed to address these areas. Management can use this list to determine the scope of the next add-on project.

Summary

Having a well-designed process for the development of a disaster recovery plan makes the process more efficient, so that it can be completed both within a reasonable period of time and within the assigned budget. During the work, the PM will likely have to deal with resource limitations, scope changes, and/or timing constraints that will result in changes (probably reductions) to the amount of work that the team can reasonably be expected to complete. These adjustments are to be expected, and will probably result in more recovery planning work being shifted forward into follow-on projects that are intended to expand the range of areas covered by the company's disaster recovery plan.

Chapter 2
When to Develop a Plan

Introduction

Which parts of a business need a disaster recovery plan? This determination should be based on hard facts about which functional areas are most essential to a business. However, many managers do not perceive the issue in this manner, instead focusing only on risk management for their favorite parts of the business, or on areas that have historically been considered to be important, but which are now significantly less so. For example, an in-house data storage system might at one time have been considered a primary risk area, but is now a much lesser risk, since the data can instead be stored in the cloud. Clearly, an evaluation is needed in order to decide when to develop a plan. In this chapter, we discuss how to identify risk areas and the need for a business impact analysis.

How to Identify Risk Areas

A good way to decide which parts of a business need a disaster recovery plan is to think about what would happen to the business if a particular function were to break down. How much would this event cost the firm? This identification process is especially valuable when a company has limited financial resources, so that it can only allocate funds to protect the highest-risk areas. This analysis is also useful when modeling the effect of a disaster that impacts all parts of a business, since management needs to decide in advance which areas will be most essential to the firm's survival.

Another way to identify high-risk areas is to probe for legal issues that might be triggered by failures within the company. If an adverse legal outcome could have a high monetary or reputational impact for the business, then these potential failures should certainly be classified as high risk.

The risk identification process can be conducted through a standard questionnaire. This questionnaire should ask the following questions for each key function:

- What does the function depend on that is sourced from outside the company?
- Is there any particular technology on which this function depends?
- How long can the function operate without any data or supplier inputs?
- How long can the function be non-operational before downstream functions are significantly impacted?
- What is the financial loss that the company will incur if the function is non-operational for one day? This loss should include lost revenues, penalties charged to the company, extra wages paid to catch up on the work after the downtime is over, and the cost of spoiled inventory.
- Will the company fall out of compliance with legal requirements if the function is non-operational? If so, what is the applicable law or regulation, and

what are the associated penalties? Would the company lose a license to operate?

- What will the impact be on customers, suppliers, and public confidence in the company if the function is non-operational?
- Which business records are most essential to the operation of the function? How are these records being protected?
- Is there any specialized equipment used by the function that could cause the function to stop if the equipment were to fail? Is there backup equipment available? If not, how long would it take to procure?

To gain full value from a questionnaire, the project team should only send it to those people most qualified to fill it out, discuss with them how it is to be completed, and then review their responses with them, to clear up any areas of uncertainty.

Another essential element of the questionnaire process is to work with each department manager in advance to create a list of the most critical functions within each department. A questionnaire should then be provided for each of these functions. The project team should track which questionnaires were issued and returned, in order to spot any instances in which questionnaires for specific functional areas are still outstanding.

Tip: Consider developing and issuing the questionnaire to a single department to ensure that it works properly, prior to rolling it out more generally throughout the company. Use as a test subject a department whose manager already supports the disaster recovery planning effort, and so will be more helpful with the testing process.

Here are several examples of high-risk areas for different types of companies:

- *Airline.* When an airline's flight reservation system goes down, it loses revenue from customers who go to the reservation systems of competing airlines instead. This also triggers a loss of customer confidence in the company.
- *Online store.* When an online store's website stops working, potential customers go elsewhere to make purchases for the duration of the outage. In addition, there is a loss of customer confidence.
- *Power company.* When a power generating station goes down for any reason, this eliminates the provision of electricity to all customers, and may also lay the company open to penalties by the applicable government regulator.
- *Restaurant.* When a restaurant's freezer fails, it loses inventory due to spoilage, as well as revenue from the meals that it can no longer serve. This also triggers a loss of customer confidence in the firm.
- *Supplier.* When a supplier of industrial parts is delivering goods to a customer on a just-in-time basis, it has to make deliveries within a two-hour time window. If it cannot reliably make these deliveries, then the customer will cancel its contract with the supplier.

> **Tip:** In cases where the people assigned to fill out questionnaires are extremely busy already, consider having a team member interview them and fill out the questionnaire on their behalf; doing so will use less of the subject's time.

EXAMPLE

In a manufacturing company, the paint shop is the bottleneck operation. If the paint shop goes down for any reason, then the company cannot complete any of its goods. Customers consider the firm's products to be time-sensitive, so if the paint shop were to go down for a day, then the company would lose $100,000, because customers would cancel their orders.

Once all questionnaires have been collected, the team summarizes them into a report that categories the criticality of all functions by department, and then returns this information to the contributing departments for a final review. This is an important step, since it allows the departments to evaluate the risk rankings of their various functions, and may result in some changes to the rankings. They may also point out functions that are missing, and for which additional questionnaires should be provided.

Business Impact Analysis

A business impact analysis (BIA) is the process of determining the criticality of business activities to ensure that operations remain resilient both during and after a business disruption. This analysis quantifies the impacts of disruptions on service delivery, so that management better understands the cost per hour of a service disruption. This analysis is also used to derive two key items, which are the recovery time objective and the recovery point objective. The *recovery time objective* (RTO) is the amount of time that a specific function can be nonoperational before the entity suffers from it. When the RTO is quite short, a firm will probably need to direct a large amount of resources at it to ensure that any downtime suffered is extremely short. Any RTOs found will probably attract the bulk of a company's risk mitigation funding. The *recovery point objective* (RPO) is the amount of data that can be lost before a company function is seriously compromised. When a function's data requirements are high, management needs to direct more resources towards risk mitigation.

EXAMPLE

A warehousing firm runs a sophisticated distribution management system (DMS), where goods being delivered to one side of a warehouse are cross-docked over to a waiting truck in a different bay of the facility. If the DMS goes down, all operations within the facility will come to an immediate halt, so its RTO is essentially zero. Further, the system will be rendered nonfunctional within one hour if it stops receiving satellite tracking data on inbound and outbound trucks; thus, its RPO is one hour.

There are several ways in which a specific aspect of a disaster can be quantified. For example, one could calculate the loss of revenue that would occur if a restaurant location were to be destroyed, or the scrap cost associated with the loss of vaccines if a hospital refrigerator were to fail, or the fees charged by the government if mandated pollution controls are not installed in a timely manner.

EXAMPLE

The Lonely Duckling Airline operates its own flight reservation system, which customers use to book flights over the Internet. If the system goes down, customers cannot book flights, and there is no manual backup system for it. Even with only a hundred flight departures per day, a BIA reveals that the company would lose $100,000 per day if the reservation system were to go down. Based on the company's current cash reserves, the airline would only be able to survive for 30 days if the reservation system were to remain out of commission for that period of time. Consequently, investing in multi-layered controls around the reservation system appears to be a significant priority for the firm.

EXAMPLE

Catenary Corporation builds bridges. It is charged a penalty of $1,000 per hour beyond the specific time and date when a bridge is supposed to be completed over the Mississippi River. Since the company could potentially lose $24,000 for every day that the bridge is late in being completed, the firm's BIA focuses on every aspect of the construction process that could cause the bridge completion to be delayed.

> **Note:** Since a BIA only provides a picture of the risk situation as of a specific point in time, it will need to be repeated at intervals, and especially when there has been a significant change to the business.

What one business considers to be its most critical functions may not be the same for another business, if the entities have different missions. For example, an integrated manufacturer of electric cars would likely determine that its mission is closely tied to the development and manufacture of batteries, while an Internet retailer would likely consider that maintaining its web store is most critical to its survival. Thus, a close examination of why a business exists is needed at the start of a BIA.

An essential advantage of conducting a BIA is delving into precisely what is needed to maintain essential business operations. For example, a review of the IT department might find that the person responsible for maintaining a bank's legacy software (coded in COBOL) is about to retire, which will leave no one in the company who understands how to make changes to it. Or, a review of the warehousing department reveals that the company supporting the firm's distribution management system is about to switch over to an entirely re-written software package – which may not mesh with the company's enterprise resources management system.

A BIA can also inform management about how long a company can continue to operate if a key function were to go down. This usually means the loss of IT systems, but consider an amusement park – how long will customers stick around if the park's premier ride goes down for maintenance? Or consider how long a ski resort can stay operational if one of its gondolas breaks down. This will depend on exactly which gondola – if it serves a large amount of terrain higher on the mountain, then it is entirely possible that the failure of one specific gondola could shut down the entire resort.

A BIA can also focus on the identification of essential corporate records, and what would happen if they were to be lost. For example, if essential accounting records for outstanding accounts receivable were to be lost, how would the company collect the balances due? Or, what would happen if a company's fixed asset records were to be lost in a disaster? Would the firm be able to justifiably file claims for reimbursement from its insurance company?

Yet another use of a BIA is identifying for management how it should allocate scarce resources to resuscitate the business if a disaster strikes. The analysis can categorize exactly which areas of the business must be funded first in the event of a catastrophe. For example, if a tornado levels a production facility, the firm may need to immediately fund an outsourcing effort to shift manufacturing elsewhere, followed by the reconstruction of a sales operation to keep the company's sales backlog full while the rest of the enterprise is rebuilt.

The business could even attempt to address more difficult quantification topics, such as the loss of sales caused by a loss of customer confidence in a key product. This is not a minor issue, since a customer death from a product failure could cause a massive, overnight decline in sales. The same issue might also lead to the departure of valuable employees from the company, not to mention the loss of suppliers who no longer want to be associated with the firm.

EXAMPLE

A provider of all-natural fruit juice drinks to health food stores hears that a customer has died from food poisoning after drinking one of the firm's bottled juices. The company is now at immediate risk of being dropped by its distributors, as well as of being fined or shut down by the Food and Drug Administration.

EXAMPLE

A chemical company inadvertently suffers a release of carcinogenic materials, which spreads to the neighboring community via groundwater contamination. The effect is a complete loss of trust by the local community, which then passes ordinances that require the firm to shut down.

How to Run a Business Impact Analysis

A BIA is part of the activities conducted by a disaster recovery planning team. It is essential to have an experienced person run the BIA portion of the project, in order to obtain reliable information about which company functions are really the most important, and their monetary effect on the organization if they fail. Department managers can become quite heated during this analysis, since they might take poorly to the concept that their departments are not especially important, or that they harbor activities that could bring down the company. Given the obvious potential for politicization of these issues, the manager needs to occupy a significantly hefty position within the firm to stave off attempts to influence the final BIA report.

Summary

The process of creating a business process analysis can be quite an educational one for a company. Managers may have to reassess their perceptions of the criticality of various business functions, and may be surprised at how much money the firm could lose if certain functions were to be shut down. Once this analysis is completed, management should have a better idea of the priorities for mitigating risk, as well as the functions that need to be restored first in the event of a disaster.

Chapter 3
How to Evaluate Risk

Introduction

Based on the activities discussed in the previous chapters, the project team should have a good idea of the functional areas that present the greatest risk to the company. It can now proceed to an evaluation of risks throughout the areas included in the project scope. In this chapter, we cover several risk-related definitions, the cost of downtime, risk layers, and risk assessment.

The Nature of Risk

Before discussing the evaluation of risk, it helps to define what we are talking about. *Risk* is the probability of a negative outcome. It is measured as how likely an event is to occur, as well as the level of damage that will be caused by it. Thus, risk is about the potential for an occurrence of something bad; as such, a possible calamity may never occur at all, or it could happen several weeks in a row.

Risk is usually assessed by evaluating historical outcomes, to determine how frequently outlier situations occur, and the effects of those events. This can be useful information when a business has been in operation for a long period of time. However, a historical orientation in a risk assessment can be dangerous, since future events may bear no relation to events that have arisen in the past.

A business may elect to completely avoid a risk. For example, the risk of destruction due to an earthquake can be nearly eliminated by moving the business to a location in which there has been no history of even the slightest earthquake. In other cases, a known risk is accepted, and instead management elects to engage in risk mitigation activities to reduce the damage, such as installing a backup power generator in a building where the power supply has historically proven to be unreliable.

What is a Disaster?

Since this book is about disaster recovery planning, it would be useful to define the concept of a disaster. According to the Red Cross, a disaster is defined as follows:

> A disaster is a sudden, calamitous event that seriously disrupts the functioning of a community or society and causes human, material, and economic or environmental losses that exceed the community's or society's ability to cope using its own resources. Though often caused by nature, disasters can have human origins.

For the purposes of this book, we are more concerned with disasters as they pertain to businesses, in which case the definition can be pared down to be any event that unexpectedly disrupts a critical business function.

The key focus of a disaster recovery plan is (predictably) disasters. These are events that have a sudden and major impact on a business. Thus, the loss of a printer in the accounting department may impede the production of customer invoices, but can hardly be considered a disaster. Conversely, when a water main breaks next to a business and drowns it in a few million gallons of water, *that* is a disaster.

The Risk Analysis

A core activity in disaster recovery planning is *risk analysis*, which is the process of identifying potential threats to an organization. This analysis begins with the identification of the key areas of the business, which we covered in the preceding chapter. We then identify the risks pertaining to those specific areas.

When developing a risk analysis, a good way to limit its range is to conduct an evaluation that spans only a specific number of years, such as from the present day through three years into the future. Doing so eliminates consideration of events that are unlikely to arise within that time frame. For example, if a company has a factory in another country and the current administration of that country is considered to be friendly to the company and will be in power for the next three years, then consideration of the risk of asset expropriation within that country can probably be eliminated. Of course, as the planning horizon rolls forward over time, this will eventually encompass the possibility of a change in administration in that country, which may call for another look at the risk of asset expropriation.

There are different costs to consider when engaged in a risk analysis. One is the cost of downtime associated with the loss of a business function. The cost of downtime includes the following elements:

- *Intangible expenses*. These expenses are usually associated with a loss of reputation. They are the most difficult to define, and yet could be the largest costs to a business over the long term. They include damage to a firm's reputation, increased employee turnover, and lost opportunities for joint ventures. These expenses can be very roughly measured by ascribing any before-and-after changes in sales, employee turnover and so forth to intangible expenses (though doing so may result in the inadvertent inclusion of other causes of revenue and expense changes in the measured outcome).
- *Late fees*. If a disaster causes a company to make late deliveries to its customers, then they may be justified in levying late fees against it.
- *Legal expenses*. Shareholders may sue a company if a disaster causes the company's share price to decline, and they believe that management was negligent in constructing adequate risk management systems to guard against any resulting losses.
- *Lost assets*. A disaster may cause an organization to lose inventory or fixed assets. The amount of this loss is their carrying amount, less any offsetting insurance payments.
- *Lost productivity*. When employees are idled by a loss of functionality, a company typically continues to pay them. Since they are being paid during a

nonproductive period, this is essentially lost productivity. It can be measured by multiplying the fully-loaded labor cost of each employee rendered useless by an outage by the total number of hours that they are unable to work.

- *Lost revenue.* When a business is unable to ship products or provide services, customers will buy from a competitor instead, which represents a loss of revenue. This is especially the case when goods or services are highly commoditized, so that customers have no reason to only buy from the company. Lost revenue is a continuing concern for any organization selling over the Internet, since potential customers can just switch to a competitor's website and buy there, instead. Lost revenue can be calculated by determining the average revenue generated per hour, and multiplying by the number of hours that a business is unable to generate revenue.
- *Penalties.* If a disaster causes a company to miss deadlines or not meet government-imposed requirements, then the government may impose penalties.
- *Shipping expenses.* A company may need to pay extra to ship goods to its customers on an overnight basis, to meet its delivery commitments established prior to the disaster. These extra costs can be teased out of the shipping expense account in the general ledger.
- *Wages expense.* The company may have to hire outside help to assist with cleanup operations, reconstruction, and/or reconstructing lost records. This information can be obtained from the temporary labor and consulting services accounts in the general ledger.

Risk Layers

When developing a risk analysis, it can be useful to consider the situation as being divided into different tranches of risk. The Level 1 tranche is any risk that can potentially close down the entire business. For example, a hurricane passing directly over company headquarters could inflict severe wind and water damage on the facility and any nearby suppliers, making it necessary to shut down. The Level 2 tranche applies only to a specific facility. For example, a local power interruption might cause one company facility to shut down, but not another one 20 miles away that is on a different power grid. Other potential causes of a Level 2 risk are earthquakes, forest fires, floods, tornadoes, and bomb threats. The Level 3 tranche applies to the data systems of the company, such as its networks and data storage systems. This risk tranche is considered to be especially important, since a data failure – such as an enterprise resources planning system going down – can impact most of the functional areas within a company. The Level 4 tranche applies to individual departments. Most disasters tend to impact individual departments, and so are more easily mitigated – though some can still bring down an entire business. Finally, the Level 5 tranche covers those risks that only apply to specific individuals. Level 5 risks are dealt with all the time by employees, who have developed risk mitigation techniques that deal with most issues that may arise. In the following sub-sections, we address each of the risk tranches in more detail.

Level 1 Tranche: Company-Wide Risks

Risks in the Level 1 tranche tend to impact broad geographical regions. Examples are an earthquake or a tsunami. These events can damage large swathes of territory, including multiple company facilities, customers, and suppliers. For example, an earthquake can cut power lines, destroy gas lines, damage roads, and level entire buildings. This type of devastation could potentially obliterate a business, because employees may not be able to come to work, local emergency services are overwhelmed, and local infrastructure has been destroyed. Risks that fall into the Level 1 tranche can be subdivided into the following general categories:

- *Natural disasters*. The applicability of natural disasters will depend on where a company is located. For example, a business situated in Oklahoma had better plan for tornadoes, while a firm located in California will be more interested in the risks posed by earthquakes and wildfires. A business situated in the upper Midwest may have a particular interest in thunderstorms or flooding, while a Florida gulf-coast company might be more interested in hurricanes, and a Montana business finds that its main interest is snow storms. Worldwide, the most damage from natural disasters is caused by flooding, since it destroys most assets and may contain pollutants and debris that need to be cleared from a facility. Most of these natural disasters are expected to become more likely as global warming effects intensify.
- *Human-caused disasters*. Actions taken by others can trigger disasters. For example, a water main break can flood a business, a trucker's chemical spill can close a facility, and local rioting could cause damage to a facility that is in the path of the rioters. More commonly, a business might be shut down due to labor disputes, or because a key supplier cannot deliver goods on time.

Level 2 Tranche: Facility-Specific Risks

Risks in the Level 2 tranche are more likely to impact a single facility. Examples are the loss of power, phone service, or Internet service into a building due to a local construction error that cuts an incoming line. All three of these examples can completely stop service to customers, resulting in a loss of sales. When evaluating the possible severity of facility-specific risks, consider the historical record of how frequently impacting events occur, when they occur, and how long each event lasted. For example, every time there has been an Internet outage, it was during working hours and lasted an average of four hours before service was restored.

Equipment malfunctions can also impact a facility. The most obvious examples are the loss of air conditioning or heat, which can have serious ramifications. For example, a loss of air conditioning during the summer can make working conditions intolerable (especially in a high-humidity environment), damage sensitive electronic equipment, and trigger the growth of mildew within a facility. The loss of heat can be even worse, since it can cause water pipes to freeze and then burst when they are reheated, causing flooding within a building. Also, any inventory items containing water may be ruined.

Facilities can be subject to varying degrees of risk relating to fire. While one might think that fires are primarily triggered within a building, the reality is that they can also arise from outside it. If the local area gets very dry during the warmer months, and especially if a facility is located in a wooded area or one surrounded by dry vegetation, then it is certainly at increased risk of damage due to fire. This risk is worsened when there are combustibles, such as pallets, stacked near a building. An additional fire concern is how far away a building is from a fire station. When a building is located in a more rural area, this distance is likely to be greater, which means that any fire has more time in which to expand, possibly consuming an entire building before help arrives.

Yet another facility-specific risk is structural flaws in a building. It may be constructed to meet all local building codes, and yet could fail under very specific circumstances. For example, winds from a tornado could tear away a roof or collapse a building, while an excess snow load on a roof could collapse it. Or, lightning strikes a building and causes a power surge, frying electronic equipment within the facility. Yet another possibility is a water pipe situated next to an exterior wall, which freezes on a cold day and then bursts, flooding part of a building.

A facility could also be at risk due to physical security issues. For example, it may need to be evacuated when a bomb threat is called in or a suspicious package is detected. Or, a disgruntled employee might attempt to sabotage the facility. Yet another possibility is some level of workplace violence that causes a facility to be evacuated.

Some Level 2 risks occur surprisingly frequently. For example, someone digging at a local construction project could easily cut through a bundle of cables leading into a company facility, thereby taking out both its phone and Internet service with one slash of a backhoe blade. There is rarely any backup cable for phone and Internet service, so a facility can be taken offline instantly. Another frequent issue is water main breakages, especially in colder climates. As the ground flexes due to freezing and thawing, the pipes buried in it flex too, and may occasionally break. When a water main breaks, the water pressure in a building drops suddenly, making it difficult or impossible to flush toilets or operate cooling systems – which can render a building uninhabitable within a few hours.

Level 3 Tranche: Data System Risks

Risk managers pay attention to data systems risks, because failures in this area can impact an entire organization. Failures can arise in multiple areas, such as when a network goes down, servers fail, hard drives crash, and data are corrupted. These risks may be enhanced at the point when more-robust systems are installed, because they must be fine-tuned to interact with the older systems that are still in place.

Of particular concern is the network, since most departments rely on it to complete basic processes, and because it is comprised of multiple components that can fail – making this a high-risk item. A network is comprised of servers (which store files and programs), clients (the computers that use the network), a network interface card located in each computer, transmission media (various types of cable that connect computers), peripherals (such as printers), a switch (which delivers messages to destinations within a network), and a network operating system that allows computers to communicate over the network. If any one of these components fails, a network can be rendered inoperable.

Another concern is computer viruses. One should consider the risk of damage if a virus infects just one computer, or spreads through the company, or is spread even further, to suppliers and/or customers. The level of this risk depends on the extent to which firewalls and virus-scanning software are used, as well as the company policy on allowing off-site use of company computers that are then plugged back into the company network.

Data theft is yet another concern. A hacker may be able to download data directly from the company's systems, or laptops could be stolen when they are taken off-site, along with all the data stored on them. This risk includes the possibility of the data finding its way into the hands of competitors, or of it being made generally available to the public. Alternatively, a hacker might encrypt the data on-site and demand a ransom in order to unlock the data; this last option could effectively stop all company operations unless the data can be recovered.

Level 4 Tranche: Departmental Risks

Departmental risks are more tightly focused than the risks stated in the higher-level tranches. These risks usually interfere only with the day-to-day running of one department. Examples are the loss of an employee, or a data file being corrupted, or a fire sprinkler being set off and ruining everything within a small area. Or, a fire may start and be confined to a single room. Some departmental risks are only associated with certain functions. For example, the loss of a refrigerator in the company cafeteria could be critical to the department's operation, as could the loss of a forklift in the warehouse or a computer-aided design workstation in the engineering department.

An additional consideration at the departmental level is the existence of any vital records within a department. The risk they present depends on the existence of backups, and how safely they are stored. This is a particular concern when records are needed to meet certain regulatory or legal requirements, or where there could be a significant downside to their loss. Records should also be considered vital when they are used in dealings with customers or suppliers, such as product plans (in the engineering department), purchase orders (in the purchasing department), or customer invoices (in the accounting department).

Level 5 Tranche: Individual Risks

The final tranche of risk pertains to the individual. These risks are similar to those identified at the department level, but are only associated with one person. For example, a maintenance person might consider that a missing tool is a risk, if it is hard to replace. Or, a financial analyst might consider that the loss of a statistical analysis software package and all associated project data would be a serious blow. Alternatively, an in-house attorney might consider the loss of confidential legal files to be a significant loss. Risks at this level do not need to be formally recognized if they can be easily corrected through the presence of duplicate equipment or personnel in the adjacent area. Thus, someone working at a computer terminal in a large accounting department would not be overly concerned if his terminal died, because there would be other replacement terminals available in the immediate area.

Risk Specificity

When evaluating risks, it can be helpful to identify the locations in which disaster occurrences are more likely to have a damaging effect on a business. For example, a fire in the dumpster outside a company facility is much less critical than one in the document storage area, and can be easily mitigated by moving the dumpster further away from the building. Similarly, flooding in the janitorial department is much less critical to company operations than one that impacts the shop floor. Specifying *where* disasters would be most damaging tells the project team where to focus its attention in terms of developing cost-effective risk mitigation activities.

Additional Sources of Information

When evaluating risk, there are some additional sources of information that might be of use. The Federal Emergency Management Agency (FEMA) maintains an excellent national flood map that can be used to ascertain whether your company facilities are located within floodplain areas. Go to www.fema.gov and access their Floods & Maps option to access the floodplain maps. FEMA also provides significantly less detailed earthquake hazard maps, which are available on the same website.

It can be useful to make inquiries with the local fire department to learn about the estimated time required for a fire truck to arrive, which may vary by time of day. The arrival time may be lengthened substantially if the department uses volunteer fire-fighters. Similarly, one might contact the local police department to gain an understanding of the types of crimes reported near company facilities, as well as their frequency and when they occur.

The information collected from these additional investigations can then be used to refine one's evaluation of various types of risk, both in terms of their severity and timing.

Assessing Risk

Once a listing of all risks has been compiled by tranche, create an estimate for each risk of how likely it is to occur within a reasonable timeline (such as three to five years), its impact on the business, and the cost to mitigate the risk. By applying a 1 to 10 ranking for each of these factors, it should be possible to narrow down the assessment to those risks that are frequent and have the most impact on the organization. Within this cluster, management will want to address those risks that are the least expensive to mitigate, since they represent the most cost-effective mitigation solutions. Risks with higher mitigation costs will be assigned a lower priority.

EXAMPLE

An email service provider is assessing its identified risks. In reviewing the risk of email service going down, it assigns the highest score of 10 to the impact on the business, a score of 3 for its frequency of occurrence, and a score of 8 to the remediation cost, which involves the construction of a backup data center.

EXAMPLE

A hard candy manufacturer is assessing its identified risks. In reviewing the risk of its candy cooker machine going down, it assigns a mid-range score of 5 to the impact on the business (since it has other cookers in service), a score of 9 to its frequency of occurrence (since the machine is old and in need of replacement), and a score of 6 to the remediation cost, which involves purchasing a replacement machine.

Summary

The evaluation of risk calls for an organized approach, where the project team works its way through a range of possibilities, starting with company-wide risks and proceeding down into risks that may only impact individual departments or a few of their employees. Once collected, one should assign severity rankings to each one for their frequency of occurrence, impact on the organization, and estimated mitigation cost. This information is used to spotlight which risks to concentrate on, and is needed in setting a risk mitigation strategy, as described in the next chapter.

Chapter 4
Recovery Strategy Formulation

Introduction

Once the tasks in the preceding chapters have been completed, the next step is to formulate a recovery strategy. This strategy provides the overall direction for how management plans to enact a disaster recovery effort. It represents a tradeoff between the cost of preparing for a disaster and the time required to recover from it. As an example, the IT function ideally would like to have a completely mirrored data processing unit, so that it can switch over to the backup in moments and continue with hardly a break. A credit card processing company may decide that it cannot afford any processing downtime at all, in which case it not only has a backup data processing unit, but also a backup to the backup. However, this is quite expensive, so management typically considers some lesser solution that trades off a lower cost against a longer recovery time. The recovery strategy states this tradeoff.

In the following pages, we cover the purpose of a recovery strategy, how it is structured, a number of recovery alternatives, and several related matters.

The Purpose of a Recovery Strategy

A recovery strategy should not be designed to restore company functions to their exact state just prior to a disaster, because doing so would be too expensive. Instead, the intent is to restore the most essential business functions to the minimum level required to attain an acceptable level of service. By attaining this minimal service level, affected functions can keep operating sufficiently well for management to then plan for a more complete restoration of pre-disaster service levels, which may require a substantially larger investment.

> **Tip:** As a side-effect of the recovery strategy formulation, it can make sense to simplify the more essential processes. Since simplified processes are also more efficient, they are easier to re-install and operate.

The restoration of essential business functions should have a particular focus on areas where a failure can bring down a business process, which typically applies to process bottlenecks. Consequently, the strategy should concentrate on positions for which there is only one qualified person available, or one piece of equipment that can complete an essential processing operation. This is especially important when a failure is visible to customers.

Structure of the Recovery Strategy

A recovery strategy should first address company-wide issues. For example, if an entire facility is impacted, the strategy should address whether the company will provide for a backup work area for employees – one that contains all the furnishings and office equipment needed for employees to continue working on critical business functions. This may need to include connections to the company's backup data center, so that staff can access key data to continue with their most important functions. Or, in the case of a pandemic, the strategy should be to set up employees to work from home, with sufficient equipment to access the company data that they need. Ultimately, the strategy focuses on how a business continues to provide goods and services to its customers, in order to keep cash flow positive. If some departments do not directly contribute to the provision of goods and services, then they are downgraded in the recovery strategy.

In addition to the company-wide issues, the strategy should also focus attention on the key areas to be addressed by each department. For example, the strategy could state that the primary focus of the accounting department is to process payroll (thereby downgrading all other activities), while the manufacturing department should focus strictly on shipping to meet existing customer orders (rather than building stock to meet expected future demand).

Recovery Point Objective

As stated earlier, the recovery point objective (RPO) is the amount of data that can be lost before a company function is seriously compromised. The concept usually applies most closely to the frequency with which data are backed up. For example, if a company incrementally backs up all data at the end of each business day, and data are corrupted late in the afternoon of the current day, then all the data originating since the last backup on the night before will be lost. If such a loss is not tolerable, then the strategy needs to state that a more frequent backup cycle must be implemented.

> **Note:** The recovery point objective is a particular concern when customer orders are entered into the system from orders placed over the phone. It is nearly impossible to reconstruct these orders if the system crashes, which calls for the use of very frequent backups.

Recovery Time Objective

As stated earlier, the recovery time objective (RTO) is the amount of time that a specific function can be nonoperational before the entity suffers from it. When the RTO is quite short, the strategy should clarify that the firm will direct the bulk of its resources toward the rapid recovery of functionality. This strategic objective is a strong indicator for how the supporting disaster recovery budget will be spent.

Recovery Site Distance

The recovery strategy should include guidelines for how far backup recovery sites are supposed to be from the firm's primary data centers. This distance rule represents a balancing act, because they need to be sufficiently far away to avoid any disasters that befall the primary data centers, while not being so distant that they are difficult for employees to access. For example, when the primary data center is located on the Florida gulf coast and so has a higher probability of being hit by a hurricane, the backup data center needs to be well away from all likely storm tracks (and probably well inland), so that the same storm is unlikely to impact the backup location.

Recovery Alternatives

The recovery strategy should specify the manner in which a business will recover its operations. This strategy will likely vary be department, since the recovery for an IT facility will be substantially different from the one employed to (for example) recover a destroyed warehousing operation.

Tip: In many companies, the first priority for a recovery strategy is to make key IT functions operational again. This must be first, because many other departments are unable to operate without access to the company network.

The most thorough recovery alternative is to recover operations at a different company location. By keeping operations in-house, a business can more precisely control all aspects of the recovery effort, typically with systems that are roughly the same as those that were lost. For example, a company that loses a warehouse to a hurricane can simply start shipping goods from the next closest company-owned warehouse.

Another alternative is paying to maintain a recovery site in a location sufficiently far away to be assured that the backup location will not be impacted by the same disaster. This approach is more commonly used for IT operations, where facilities need to be maintained that meet the company's environmental, infrastructure, data storage, and software requirements. This facility should use a different power grid than the one used by the main company operation, to reduce the risk of the same disaster bringing down its operations. There are several variations on this concept, which are as follows:

- *Application service provider.* This involves off-site storage of all software and data, where users can log in from any location. This approach allows for immediate access to the system from anywhere, as long as users can gain access to a computer and a telecommunications link. This approach is not expensive, and shifts a significant proportion of the disaster recovery planning burden over to the service provider.
- *Cold site.* This is an empty computer room, which the company will have to populate with equipment and load with data from the last backup conducted. It is a lower-cost option, but will require a lengthy recovery time. It works well for entities that do not rely heavily on their data centers.

- *Hot site.* This is a computer room in which a sufficient amount of equipment is in place, and into which the latest backup can be loaded. This is a much more expensive option, and will still require several days to bring back on line.
- *Mirrored site.* This is a duplicate of the main data center that mirrors all data storage. It is an extremely expensive option, but allows for nearly immediate IT system recovery. This is the option of choice for larger companies that cannot afford to have a prolonged IT outage.

A final option is to lease space immediately after a disaster has struck, and restart operations from there. This usually means that the replacement space will only have basic wiring, utilities, and infrastructure, and the company will have to rebuild all other facilities from there. This may require a fairly lengthy recovery interval. For example, if the accounting department is using accounting systems that are located in the cloud, it could theoretically just install new computers at a leased location and re-access the cloud to bring its systems back on-line.

> **Note:** When electing to lease space after a disaster has occurred, keep in mind that the bottleneck impacting the new space is likely to be obtaining adequate Internet access. Depending on the supply and demand situation for the Internet provider, it could take weeks to have adequate bandwidth installed.

A variation on the concept of leasing office space is to lease an office trailer. These are preconfigured trailers with their own power generators and satellite Internet connections, which can be positioned anywhere that the company wants. While expensive to lease, they provide an immediate solution for the most critical company functions. However, any units available locally may be snapped up by other parties in the event of a regional disaster.

When considering recovery alternatives, keep in mind that they only need to be sufficient for those people needed to provide the minimum level of service – not a complete replication of the company's facilities prior to the disaster. This means that all other employees can be encouraged to work from home. They can be set up with a virtual private network (which is easily available as a downloaded application from many providers) on their home computers, and can then use this secure form of access to connect to the company network.

> **Tip:** When it is essential to conduct as much work as possible from an organized company location, consider adding a second shift for those employees who are not directly customer-facing (such as accounting, finance, engineering, and legal), who can take over the work spaces abandoned by the customer-facing people (sales, marketing, and customer service) who have just finished working the first shift.

SAMPLE RECOVERY STRATEGY

Luminescence Corporation operates a floodlight manufacturing facility. Its recovery strategy is as follows:

- Administrative staff will operate from the training facility at company headquarters, which is located 10 miles away. There are training computers for every seat in the training facility, with Internet access. The training facility has sufficient space for 1/3 of the administrative staff. All other administrative staff will be encouraged to work from home via virtual private network connections.
- Since all software and data are managed in the cloud by an application service provider, people positioned at the training facility will have access to all company records as soon as they sign in.
- Executive staff will rent out short-term office space at a local office space rental center, with sufficient access to conference rooms.
- A one-month finished goods reserve of fluorescent bulbs will be maintained at all times. This will allow the purchasing staff enough time to outsource production to a third party until the main facility can be brought back online.
- The disaster recovery plan administrator is responsible for periodically reviewing the finished goods buffer to ensure that a one-month reserve is maintained. The administrator is also responsible for ensuring that the computers and Internet connections at the training facility are adequate, and for conducting annual tests to ensure that this is the case.

The expectation is for administrative staff at the training facility to be back in operation within one business day of a disaster, while work-from-home staff should be operational within two business days.

Pandemic Strategy

As has been made quite clear during the COVID-19 crisis, a separate pandemic strategy is needed for all businesses, since pandemics have a global impact on not only a company, but also its entire supplier base and customers. The focus of this strategy is to minimize the spread of the disease over an extended period of time, since a vaccine or other cure may take several years to be developed and tested before it can be released. The strategy may need to encompass the following items:

- Configure the company sick leave policy to keep employees from having to work in the office while sick. A good approach is to eliminate the cap on sick days for the duration of the pandemic.
- Have as many employees as possible work from home, using a virtual private network to access company systems online.
- Mandate frequent deep cleans of company work spaces to eliminate any viruses brought in by workers.
- Mandate home quarantines for employees who have traveled in areas where infection rates are high.

- Provide adequate personal protective equipment to all employees who come into contact with others.
- Provide hand sanitation throughout all company facilities.
- Switch to video conferencing for company meetings, as well as meetings with outside parties.

Summary

A recovery strategy is generally focused on investing just enough to avoid having a disaster completely shut down a business. It should be able to bring functionality back to a basic level, from which management can then determine how to invest funds to achieve a more complete recovery. The strategy should provide a sufficient amount of high-level guidance to clarify the recovery level that is expected. In particular, it should specify how quickly the business should take to return to a basic level of functionality, since this requirement drives the overall cost of the recovery effort.

Chapter 5
Initial Enhancements

Introduction

It takes a number of months to develop a detailed disaster recovery plan. So, what can be done in the meantime to give some protection to a business? In this chapter, we cover the most essential information that should be collected in order to enhance a firm's ability to recover from a disaster right now. Each section of this chapter summarizes a specific set of information that can be of great assistance in dealing with a disaster in the short term.

Key Personnel

A call list should be created for each type of disaster that can be reasonably foreseen. When a disaster occurs, the call list relating to it is not just the department manager most immediately impacted by it. Instead, several additional people may need to be contacted, such as the firm's legal counsel, public relations director, facilities manager, and chief executive officer – the contact list depends on the nature of the disaster. Much of this information can be sourced from an organization chart, which details who is responsible for what within the company. If the chart is out of date, then an initial task is to create an updated version.

EXAMPLES

The accounting software for the payroll system crashes. The call list for this issue includes the payroll manager, controller, and human resources manager.

An employee falls off a ladder in the warehouse and is injured. The call list for this issue includes 911, the warehouse manager, the human resources manager, and legal counsel.

A pipe bursts and floods the basement. The call list for this issue includes the fire department, facilities manager, and chief executive officer.

In addition to these call lists, assemble a listing of the home phone numbers for all employees. This is needed for two reasons. First, if there is a major disaster that requires employees to stay home, there needs to be a central listing of this information in order to contact them. And second, if a disaster calls for the specialized services of a particular employee, the company can get in touch with this person during off-hours periods.

Tip: If the company has people with similar skill sets in other locations, collect their contact information, too. Their expertise may be needed to deal with recovery issues.

EXAMPLE

A company's warehouse management system goes down and cannot be rebooted. The in-house expert who normally deals with this issue is currently hiking across Antarctica and so is extremely inaccessible. The backup person occupies the same position at a subsidiary, which operates the same software.

Service Arrangements

Some services are so specialized that it is more cost-effective to hire an outside expert on an as-needed basis to make repairs, rather than having an in-house expert on the payroll. For example, organizations typically pay for service contracts for their standard off-the-shelf software, as well as for copiers, printers, HVAC, network equipment and software, and specialized production equipment. Be sure to collect the contact information for each of these suppliers, along with the company's relevant contract and customer numbers, so that they can be readily reached in the event of an emergency. Having one's customer number readily available may be especially important, since some suppliers use it to verify the existence of a service contract.

The listing of service providers should include the name of the company's designated contact person for each supplier. This may be needed when suppliers have requested that service calls always originate from these people.

> **Tip:** Conduct a walkthrough of the facility and make inquiries about service related to all major assets. Also, peruse the accounts payable records to ascertain the names of any vendor payments recorded in the repairs and maintenance account, to see if they are associated with any service arrangements.

When constructing the list of contacts, keep in mind that there may be several contacts at each supplier, such as a dedicated technician, an after-hours number to call, and a customer service number.

The contact list should also note for each supplier the hours of support under the applicable service contract. If the company wants the supplier to make a service call outside of these hours, the supplier will bill the company a hefty fee for this added service. Having the hours of support information readily available reduces of risk of unnecessarily incurring extra expenses.

> **Tip:** Make note of the date on which every service agreement expires, so that steps can be taken to renew them in an orderly manner.

When a service arrangement applies to a specific piece of equipment, consider writing the supplier and related contact information on a laminated card and posting it next to (or on) the equipment. Doing so simplifies the task of getting immediate support for an equipment failure.

> **Tip:** When attaching supplier contact information to equipment, also remove any advertising stickers for other repair organizations that may be attached to the equipment. Since the company does not have a service contract with these other parties, it would have to pay extra to use them.

In addition to documenting supplier arrangements for maintenance issues, it also makes sense to document the contact information for any suppliers of critical materials and supplies to the company. This makes it easier to procure a selection of important items (such as toner cartridges) that may be needed on short notice. Similarly, create a contact list for every utility company that services the organization, including power, water, gas, and Internet access. In addition, append a listing of the phone numbers for the nearest ambulance service, fire station, and hospital, as well as the police.

Access Rights

Access to certain areas and key assets of the company should be restricted, in order to minimize the risk of theft or damage. This means that physical locks have been installed in several parts of a business. For example, the server room is likely to be locked, as is the records room, tool crib, and spare parts room. If there is an issue in any of these areas, you will need to know who has the applicable keys, in order to gain access. This means documenting where locks are located, where keys are located, and who is authorized to use them.

> **Tip:** Ensure that the human resources department retrieves keys from anyone who has left the company, and documents the names of the replacement people who are now responsible for these keys.

Over time, keys may be lost for a variety of reasons, making it difficult to gain access to some areas. To guard against this, maintain a locked cabinet where key copies are stored. It can make sense to maintain one of these cabinets in each department, so that people can gain access to sensitive areas and assets more quickly in the event of a disaster.

> **Tip:** Obtain the contact information for several local locksmiths who are available during extended hours, in case a key cannot be found.

Buy bolt cutters for every department. They can be used not only to break company locks on an emergency basis, but also personal locks that employees have installed within the facility.

As was the case with keys, it may be necessary to maintain a listing of system passwords. These passwords are sometimes used to shut down computer systems on an emergency basis. Given the sensitive nature of these passwords, they should be kept in a locked location.

Asset Identification

The locations of several types of assets should be documented, along with some associated items of information, as noted in the following sub-sections.

Physical Assets

As part of the initial enhancement process, create a listing of all major assets within the organization, noting the name of the manufacturer, the model and serial number, and location. This means walking through each department and itemizing assets that are bottlenecks, which are expensive, or which require long lead times to replace. The most difficult assets to identify on this list are the items requiring long lead times to replace, since this may not be obvious. Whoever is in charge of purchasing for each department is in the best position to know which assets represent the most difficult replacement problems.

It can also be useful to add to the listing of major assets the names and contact information of their manufacturers, with a particular emphasis on their service departments. Doing so shortens the time needed for someone to find the correct contact when a machine has failed and requires immediate servicing.

A side benefit of conducting a department-by-department search is looking around for equipment spare parts that have been hoarded locally. When found, shift these parts into a central location and lock them up. Doing so has several benefits. First, it keeps the company from investing in too many spare parts. Second, by tracking them centrally, it is less likely that the company will buy parts that it will never use. And finally, centralized storage makes it easier to find spares when needed.

While conducting an asset investigation project, make inquiries about the last time when preventive maintenance was conducted on each asset. The focus should be on those assets that require a regular preventive maintenance program in order to operate properly. By tracking preventive maintenance, one can identify assets that are more likely to fail, which may cause a cascading series of problems.

> **Tip:** If preventive maintenance is being conducted by a service provider and the equipment fails, the company may have a claim against the service provider in the amount of the remediation expenses incurred.

Another side project in an asset investigation is to locate the user manual for each major equipment item. This manual should be stored in an obvious location near the equipment, to make it more easily accessible.

Software Assets

A description of the key software assets of a business should be compiled in the same manner as was just described for physical assets. This means asking computer users about the most essential software that they use, and summarizing for this software the names and contact information of the developers, along with the version numbers of the installed software. In addition, if the software was delivered on a physical device such as a CD or a hard drive, store it in a centralized, secure location, and maintain a separate inventory record of what has been stored there.

Hazardous Assets

A business may store a variety of hazardous chemicals and gases on the premises. When this is the case, find out exactly where they are located, how they are stored, and who is responsible for them. This information is needed both in order to direct people *toward* these items in order to secure them, as well as to keep all others *away* from them.

Emergency Assets

In a disaster, it makes sense for everyone to know where the emergency equipment is located, such as fire extinguishers, first aid kits, portable pumps, and water shutoff valves. This itemization should state exactly where the assets are located, as well as how to access them if they are located in secure places.

Another type of emergency asset is employee skills. Consider developing a skills inventory for everyone working on-site at a facility. Examples are people who work as volunteer firefighters and emergency medical technicians. Other skills that may be of use are carpentry, plumbing, and electrical. Try to maintain every possible type of rapid response contact number for these people, in order to get them on-site as quickly as possible to deal with emergencies.

Initial Audit

A good way to assess a company's initial readiness for a disaster is to visit each functional area in turn and make inquiries about the basic informational needs just noted. The key item to look for is the extent to which this information is readily available. If it is scattered about and requires a substantial amount of time to collect, then there is room for improvement. Also, if the information is being collected in a rush from multiple sources, a reasonable question to ask is whether it can be relied upon. Whenever the information is poorly organized, that function should be targeted for the project team's immediate attention to address the indicated shortcomings.

Disaster Recovery Priorities

It can be helpful to create a list that states the order of priority for the essential services that are to be restored first within the company, and which can be restored later. For example, restoring power is likely to be the number one priority, since few functional areas can operate without it. The exact priority will vary by company. For example, when a facility has been completely wiped out by a tsunami, rebuilding it from scratch is probably not the main priority. Instead, shifting computer systems to an application service provider and setting up employees to work from home may be the core priority items. Conversely, a retail entity that must sell from its existing location might prioritize structural issues first (such as ensuring that the roof is stable) and then worrying about the power. In short, the disaster recovery priority will depend on the nature of the anticipated disaster and how the organization operates.

Organizing the Information

The initial information collected from each functional area should be properly organized. A good starting point is to create a divider for each functional area in a binder.

> **Tip:** Whenever information is received, attach a note to it that states the sender's contact information. This is useful when you have clarification questions.

The information received should be validated, as well as organized. This means calling all contact numbers to ensure that they go to the right person, and that these individuals are still responsible for the indicated areas.

Once the information has been collected and validated, organize it into a report, using consistent formatting throughout, and issue it to the department managers. The document should have an "as of" date clearly stated on its cover, so that managers can differentiate it from subsequent issuances. Also, consider marking the report as confidential, since it contains the home phone numbers of some employees.

> **Tip:** Maintain a mailing list of who has received the report, so that the same group can be issued updates. Also, whenever there is a position change, update the mailing list to include whoever has now become responsible for functional areas.

In addition to the department managers, the report should be stored where it is accessible by the after-hours guard.

Summary

The discussion in this chapter focused on the development of essential information for dealing with emergencies. The key concepts were understanding who to call, which suppliers can provide assistance, how to gain access to restricted areas, and knowing which assets to protect. This information should be summarized into a disaster response booklet for distribution to those assigned responsibility for dealing with disasters.

Chapter 6
The Disaster Recovery Plan

Introduction

In scuba diving, an essential rule is to plan the dive and then dive the plan. In other words, plot out what to do, and then make sure that you do it. A disaster recovery plan is the same – plan for what might happen, and then use the plan if a disaster occurs. It may not be possible to predict the exact nature of a disaster, but it should be possible to identify the basic steps to follow for several types of possible situations. Thus, the recovery steps for a production facility will probably be about the same if there is hail damage, flooding, or a fire. The intent is to reduce the amount of chaos normally associated with a disaster by providing some guidance about how to contain the problem and then recover from it.

In this chapter, we cover the four basic components of a disaster recovery plan, which are the administrative plan, technical recovery plan, work area recovery plan, and pandemic management plan, along with several related issues.

Writing the Plan

A disaster recovery plan can be a lengthy and detailed document, which might initially appear to be a formidable writing project. To make the task more manageable, first develop recovery plans for each individual department, and then combine them into a comprehensive plan for the entire organization. This will require one to compare the various departmental plans to see if they conflict with each other, and iron out these differences in the comprehensive plan.

To make the plan easier to read, the project team should adopt a standard format to be used for all aspects of it. Consider using the following best practices:

- *Font*. Keep the font size fairly large, such as 14 point, so that someone in a hurry can read the text. In addition, it is easier to read headers that are formatted in the Ariel font and paragraph text in Times New Roman font.
- *Page numbers*. Include a page number in the footer section on each page. Otherwise, there is a risk that someone might skip or lose a page when following a procedure.
- *Date*. Include the plan date in the header or footer section on each page. This tells users if they have the most recent version.
- *Format*. Each section of the plan that covers a process should begin with a *brief* description of what is being covered (remember, the reader will be in a hurry). Then note the name and contact information for the person who is primarily responsible for supporting the process, in case the reader needs to stop right there and make a call. Then note the primary customer of the process, so that the reader's next step is to contact that party to let them know that something is wrong. Only then should the document state the actions to

take. Thus, the document is designed to *first* identify the process, *then* communicate that there is a problem, and *then* fix the problem.

- *Pictures*. Where possible, supplement the text with graphics showing the location of key items, such as water shutoff valves. When the reader is in a hurry, pictures convey far more information than text, and within a shorter period of time.
- *Actions to take*. As just noted in the discussion of the format, the last item is to state the actions to take. This section should be subdivided into the following three areas:
    - o *Immediate activities*. These are the actions to be taken right now to deal with the current problem. Examples are applying immediate first aid to a heart attack victim or evacuating employees when there is a fire.
    - o *Suppression activities*. These are the actions needed to reduce the extent of the damage. For example, if there is flooding, move the most valuable assets and records to a higher floor of the building. Or, if the power fails, shut down non-essential computer equipment so that the more essential items can continue running on the firm's backup batteries.
    - o *Recovery activities*. These are the actions needed to bring services back to a minimum acceptable level. For example, a customer service center sets up a replacement call center in an empty storefront in a nearby shopping mall.

EXAMPLE

An unexpected conjunction of weather events unexpectedly drops six feet of snow on a production facility located in a rural area in northern Wisconsin. The immediate activities to deal with this event are to call in extra snow plows, and bring in bedding and food for those employees who cannot leave. The key suppression activity is to get people on the roof to clear off snow, to keep the roof from caving in. The main recovery activity is to contact customers to let them know that their deliveries may be delayed for a few days, and to contract with a local air carrier to fly selected shipments of company goods from a nearby airfield to those customers most in need of the company's products.

Do not expand the text beyond the stage of describing the steps needed to achieve a minimal acceptable service level. Once that point is reached, management can be relied upon to continue the process, developing plans to provide more complete service levels. Stopping at this point greatly reduces the amount of text in the plan.

It can be useful to insert triggering events into the plan. When something happens that has a decent probability of indicating a disaster, then an initial set of actions should be taken to prepare for it. For example, when severe thunderstorms in the area tend to cause localized flooding, it might be useful to start filling sandbags as soon as the related weather bulletin is released. Or, if an ice storm is forecast, this triggers a review of emergency supplies, on the assumption that some employees will be living on the premises until road conditions improve.

It might be worthwhile to include manual workarounds in the plan for key activities that need to be completed in the near term. For example, restoring a limited amount of power might be possible by buying a small gas-powered generator at the local home supply store. Or, employees may be allowed to use company procurement cards to buy goods for the company with no upper limit on the amount that can be spent, rather than having to wait for purchase orders. Manual workarounds tend to be expensive, so evaluate their cost-effectiveness before inserting them into the plan.

> **Tip:** For highly specific recovery issues, summarize them on laminated cards and post them in the rooms where they are most likely to be needed. For example, a card in the chemical storage room could state what to do if someone gets specific chemicals in his eyes.

When the first draft of the plan is complete, review it from the viewpoint of someone who is not an expert. It is quite possible that the experts will not be on-site when a disaster strikes, so implementing the plan will fall to someone with notably less knowledge of key functional areas. The plan needs to be written with this person in mind, so it may be useful to run through the plan with a non-expert, to see if the level of detail or textual clarity is adequate. A good choice for this person is a security guard, since there is an excellent chance that the disaster will occur well away from normal working hours, when the guard may be the only person on the premises. After all, earthquakes do not always happen been 9 a.m. and 5 p.m.

> **Tip:** Conduct tests of the plan under the assumption that key people are not on the premises, and then observe how well everyone else deals with the plan.

The plan should be stored securely in an off-site document repository. Off-site storage is needed, because the on-site location may be destroyed in a disaster. A key point is to store the plan with access permissions enabled. By doing so, an unauthorized person cannot access and alter the plan, perhaps in ways that could seriously interfere with a real disaster recovery.

The Administrative Plan

The administrative plan shows how a firm's overall disaster recovery plan is conducted. It is intended to be a reference for anyone attached to the recovery team, where they can access essential information – irrespective of which other aspects of the disaster recovery plan that they may be involved in. The main components of this plan are as follows:

- *Program charter*. This signed document states the commitment of senior management to the disaster recovery plan. It can be useful to produce the program charter when a department manager is denying the team his or her cooperation in developing and testing the plan.

- *Scope.* The scope document clarifies the boundaries of the project, so that everyone understands what is and is not included in its remit. This document will typically clarify which business functions and locations are covered by the plan.
- *Responsibilities.* These are statements of what each position associated with the program is responsible for. It is useful for clarifying which position is responsible for which tasks. A responsibilities listing can also be used to gain a better understanding of the skills needed to be effective in each role, which may drive a series of training activities to enhance the knowledge of those involved in the program. The positions addressed by these responsibility statements should include the following:

  - o *Business continuity manager.* This person is responsible for all planning and recovery activities, including strategy development, employee education, and overseeing the writing and testing of the plan.
  - o *Technical recovery manager.* This person is highly knowledgeable in information technology issues, and coordinates all activities related to the IT recoveries. This person should understand the weaknesses in current IT systems, in order to spotlight which areas are most in need of a recovery plan. This person is expected to be on-site during a system recovery, coordinating the activities of the various parties engaged in technical recovery work.
  - o *Work area recovery manager.* This person is well-versed in how company processes are set up and function, and works with departments as they develop work area recovery plans. This person is also responsible for maintaining and testing the operability of all recovery sites used by the business.
  - o *Pandemic manager.* This person is responsible for educating employees about the nature of pandemics, and how to deal with them with enhanced social distancing, personal protective equipment, sanitation procedures, and so forth. The pandemic manager also works with the rest of the team to devise plans that minimize contact not only between employees, but also with suppliers and customers.

- *Recovery strategy.* This is the strategy that we described earlier in the book, noting the general approach to be used in recovering from disasters. The strategy to be applied to each of the other planning areas (technical recovery, work area recovery, and pandemic management) should be stated.
- *Risk assessment.* This is the risk assessment that we described earlier in the book, noting the threats most likely to impact the organization and how they are to be mitigated.
- *Testing strategy.* The plan outlines the process to be used for testing each portion of the plan. It also states the trigger points (usually process changes) that will trigger updates to the plan, and therefore testing of the updates.

- *Program awareness*. An employee awareness campaign is clarified within the plan. It is designed to educate employees about the existence of the plan, who is responsible for what elements of it, and how to access the plan. Activities listed in the plan to enhance program awareness include the use of a periodic disaster recovery newsletter, posters, informational discussions at the department level, and stories about the program in the company newsletter.
- *Reference section*. The plan acts as a central repository of a variety of reference information, such as employee call lists and contact information for service providers and emergency services; this makes the plan a useful reference source for communications information. In order to be useful, the reference section may need to be updated more frequently than the rest of the administrative plan.

In short, the administrative plan outlines the framework for how the entire disaster recovery plan is supposed to work, covering material that applies to all of the more detailed recovery plans (as described next). It states the program scope, who is supposed to do what, the strategy for doing so, and where to find key information. Given its broad coverage, it is the most widely distributed of the various recovery plans.

Technical Recovery Plans

The most intensively used of all the recovery plans is the technical recovery plan, because it provides detailed instructions for how to rebuild a specific technical function, such as restoring email or cloud access to crucial company files. Since these plans are highly specific, a separate one should be written for each key technical area. To keep the number of these plans down to a reasonable amount, the project team will need to decide which specific functions are actually critical to the recovery of the business. The areas covered will likely include the most essential IT functions, those functions that directly support service to customers, telephone and Internet access, and basic utilities.

Each technical recovery plan assumes that a specific process is non-operational, and so must provide a highly-specific set of steps to bring it back to an operational status. Given the level of knowledge needed to develop these plans, the only people who can realistically write them are the people directly involved with them on a day-to-day basis. Since these people are unlikely to be well-versed in writing procedures, the project team will need to assist them with standard templates and coaching to ensure that the resulting plans are adequate.

It can be difficult to create and subsequently update technical recovery plans. They can only be written by a few highly knowledgeable people within the company, who are already quite busy with other tasks. To ensure that the plans are written, the project sponsor may need to step in to force the issue, so that the responsible parties block out sufficient time for the writing task. This is a particular concern when there is only one technical person who knows how something works, and wants to harbor his or her knowledge in order to maintain job security.

> **Tip:** A particular concern with recovery plans for IT systems is maintaining up-to-date passwords for the plans. This will require a weekly password update procedure, or an enterprise password management system that stores all passwords in the cloud.

The basic content of a technical recovery plan should include the following items:

- *Scope.* Describe what the system does and does not support. This information is needed so that the reader can discern whether the system to be recovered is the correct one for the user's needs. For example, a server may only be backing up sales data, not accounting data.
- *Functionality.* Note what the system does; again, so that the reader can decide whether the system will address what the user wants to recover.
- *Dependencies.* This is an itemization of the systems on which this recovery plan depends. For example, specific servers may need to be brought back on line before a computer system can be returned to its full operational status.
- *Support staff.* List the names of the people who can provide technical support for the system, including their home phone numbers. These people may be called upon to assist with the recovery process.
- *End users.* List the names of the people who are the primary users of this system, along with their contact information. They are in the best position to know if a system has been adequately recovered.
- *Media access.* If a recovery requires the restoration of media, then the plan must state where the most recent backup is located, who is authorized to use it, and any pass codes needed to do so.
- *Recovery steps.* Itemize the specific actions that must be taken to restore the system. It is useful to have a backup support person walk through these steps to see how understandable they are, since the resident expert may not be available to perform the actual recovery.
- *Testing process.* State the process used to test a recovered process. Typically, this means that the person who restored the process conducts a cursory review, after which an expert user conducts a more thorough feature review to ensure that everything is working (especially interfaces). After these tests, the application is opened for general use.

> **Tip:** Include photos and screen shots of recovery steps in the recovery plan, when doing so clarifies the steps to be taken.

It is impractical to develop a listing of recovery steps so detailed that absolutely anyone could perform them; the result would be too long. A better option is to assume that the person implementing the recovery has a reasonable knowledge of the underlying technology.

Another part of the technical recovery plan is a Gantt chart that shows the expected sequence and timing of recovery tasks. This is especially useful for longer recovery plans, or a set of plans that are likely to be required in response to a specific disaster (such as flooding of the server room). This chart can be used by the technical recovery manager to report on the stage that a recovery operation has reached, and the expected amount of time remaining to reach a designated completion point. It can also be used to predict the impact of delays in the recovery process on the completion of remaining tasks. This Gantt chart is devised during the testing of recovery plans, and so should provide a reasonable approximation of the amount of time required to complete a recovery plan.

> **Tip:** For multi-day recoveries, publish a rest plan that states when each person is scheduled to have downtime for sleep. Otherwise, the team will work too long, and everyone will run out of energy at about the same time.

A useful addition to the technical recovery plans is a recovery activity log, which the technical recovery manager uses to record the start and completion times for all technical recovery activities, as well as calls that were made to obtain additional resources. This is useful for analysis of the group's performance after the fact, so that the recovery plan can be improved upon.

> **Tip:** Obtain advance authorization for the technical recovery manager to have a significant amount of purchasing authority, to ensure that the need for larger expenditures is not delayed by purchasing bureaucracy.

When recovery operations are expected to be conducted at a specific offsite area, consider creating a listing of hotels and restaurants in that area. In particular, explore which restaurants will deliver food to the recovery site, and preferably during extended hours.

Recovery plans should include a communications policy, which states how frequently progress is to be reported back to the recovery command center. The policy usually mandates hourly reporting intervals, where the current restoration task is reported, as well as the estimated time to complete, additional resources needed, and who is currently engaged in the recovery effort.

The Work Area Recovery Plan

A work area recovery plan describes how to set up temporary operations for core employees at a new location. This usually involves setting up office space, but could involve more complex operations, such as manufacturing processes or a replacement retail location. These operations need to be sufficient to maintain a minimum level of service to customers, thereby protecting the firm's reputation. To maintain such service, work areas may be needed to house accounting, sales, customer service, and production personnel, as well as all related equipment (information technology was covered in the previous section).

It is essential to have a work area recovery plan, because areas outside of the IT area are less well-protected, and so are more likely to be damaged during a disaster. For example, a computer room may be protected with cinderblock walls, a backup generator, and fire suppression systems, while the firm's office space is situated

elsewhere in a lower-quality building, with no power backup and much less ability to avoid damage from any number of causes.

> **Note:** A particular concern with temporary office space is security. These areas tend to have significantly less security that a firm's permanent quarters, so there is increased risk of theft – both of information and tangible property – from the premises. This may call for an increased security presence in the area.

The requirements of a work area recovery plan will vary, depending on which department is impacted. The following bullet points describe work area recovery issues that are unique to specific groups:

- *Accounting department.* The accounting department continually works with the accounting software and supporting records. To continue doing so, they must transfer to a dedicated location with adequate file storage, and access to the accounting system. These tasks can be mitigated by using an application service provider that maintains the software over an Internet connection.
- *Customer service department.* Shifting the customer service staff to a new location is one of the more difficult tasks, because their job is to respond to inbound call traffic. Accordingly, they will need to switch to a pre-wired structure at which telephone connections can be set up quickly.
- *Executive office.* The senior management team is usually the easiest group to move, since they can transfer to a rented conference room in a hotel or a temporary office rental space, and work from their cell phones.
- *Production.* The manufacturing group is perhaps the most difficult to shift to a new location, given its use of production equipment. One option is to only re-create assembly operations, which requires less equipment. Another option is to bypass this department, except for quality control, and outsource the work instead.
- *Sales department.* The sales department can work from any location (and frequently does, if salespeople are on the road). Their main concern is getting access to email and sales data for products, such as sales proposals. This is best dealt with by storing departmental sales data in the cloud, so that they can access it anywhere.

> **Tip:** Work area recovery planning for an entire company represents an extremely broad scope. To narrow it down, identify the specific problem being solved, and only create a plan for that targeted area. This may result in a recovery plan that only deals with a small percentage of the total staff.

Based on the preceding tip, the recovery plan should state how many seats are needed in the alternative area, how far away it should be, and how soon it must be operational.

The essential requirements of a work area recovery plan are as follows:

1. *Select a recovery site.* There are several considerations relating to the selection of a recovery site. One is that functions with more specialized requirements (such as customer service) may need to operate from a specialized facility, with everyone else working from a more generic location. Another is the distance from the original company location, since it must be far enough away to avoid the disaster that struck the main facility. Yet another consideration is whether the recovery space will be acquired in advance of any disasters, or on a rush basis afterwards. Other concerns include the need for storage space, loading docks, parking, and access to public transportation.

Tip: For a multi-location company, the best recovery site could be another company location, since it is pre-configured and may have access to the same software and data used by the staff at the affected location.

2. *Assign staff.* It is quite possible that only a small minority of employees will be assigned to the recovery site, with everyone else working from home. Only those that need ready access to printed files, secure records, and office or production equipment should be assigned to the recovery site, as well as those that need to work together in teams.
3. *Equip the site.* If the site is being set up in advance of a disaster, then determine how many seats need to be configured with all necessary equipment and communications lines (with sufficient bandwidth), so that someone can use them to immediately return to work. Other seats may be preconfigured with office furniture but no equipment, on the assumption that a day or so is allowable for procuring these items. And finally, some of the area could be empty office space, requiring several days to configure. It can take a surprisingly long time to fully configure empty office space, so think carefully about how much of it to use.

Tip: Decide upon a standard equipment configuration for each office worker, so that the company can acquire a supply of computers, printers, printer cartridges, phones, and so forth. Also, acquire a few extra units of everything, in case there are equipment failures. In addition, preload computers with the firm's standard software configuration and hardware drivers, since this is a fairly slow process that might otherwise delay the recovery effort.

4. *Test the site.* Any preconfigured site must be tested to ensure that it operates as intended. Tests are also useful for the facility preparation crew, which needs practice in how to activate the site. It can also be useful to assign a few observers from each department to these tests, so that they can be familiarized with the activation process, where they will be located, and the infrastructure available to them.
5. *Activate the site.* Site activation begins with a notification to a facility preparation crew, which is responsible for facility activation. This group activates a plan to turn on heat and power, turn on phone and Internet connections, and

verify that all employees have access to company software and data. This can take several days during a disaster, when the local public utility companies are trying to restore services for the affected area. This concern is reduced when the recovery site is situated a reasonable distance away from the main facility.

6. *Operate the site.* Site operation should be driven by a list of restoration priorities, which should be clearly communicated to all employees. This list ensures that the staff is working on the highest-priority items first.

> **Tip:** For a larger facility, develop a seating chart and telephone list, so that employees can contact each other more easily. Also, label doors, offices, desks and storage cabinets, since this space will be new to everyone.

7. *Maintain the site.* Any recovery site must be maintained so that it matches the capabilities of the facility that it is supporting. In particular, verify whether the computer hardware and/or software need to be upgraded, whether the amount of bandwidth is sufficient, and whether the amount of headcount for which the site was planned is still correct. Another useful maintenance activity is to conduct occasional employee tours through it, so that employees remain familiar with what the site is supposed to do.

The work area recovery plan should include a proposed floor plan. This plan can be used to search for and build out appropriately-sized office space. The impacted departments should be involved in the floor plan design, since they might not choose to use a layout that does not work for them.

> **Tip:** Allocate a reasonable amount of square footage to each person in the recovery site. This is needed to maintain productivity levels at a time when it is especially important for employees to be productive in maintaining company operations.

Waiting to acquire space after a disaster has occurred has multiple downsides. If the disaster covers a wide area, there will be a general scramble for available space, making it difficult to obtain space at all. Also, the recovery process is a mad scramble, since it is impossible to develop a work area recovery plan when there is no area in which to locate it. And finally, it can take an inordinate amount of time to equip and activate the site, since it requires the immediate support of a number of service providers – which may not be readily available. These issues are noted in the following table, which summarizes the advantages and disadvantages of the various recovery options.

Advantages and Disadvantages of Recovery Options

Site Option	Advantages	Disadvantages
No prepared site	Very low cost until it is needed	No control over the location, requires lengthy ramp-up, difficult to develop a work area recovery plan
Trailer-based work space	Can locate anywhere, can activate within a day	Expensive to rent, may have to rent space in which to position it, limited to the capabilities of the equipment in the trailer
Use another company location	Very secure, known equipment and bandwidth capabilities, quick activation	Available capacity could be low, may be far away
Use separate hot site	Very secure, known equipment and bandwidth capabilities, quick activation	Very expensive

The Pandemic Management Plan

A *pandemic* management plan specifies how to keep company functions operating in the event of a pandemic. The unique feature of this plan is that it must describe an alternative operating path for the company that may last for one or two years, as opposed to the more temporary nature of other recovery plans.

The key point underlying a pandemic management plan is to minimize contact with people. Contact reduction not only between employees, but between employees and all others is essential. This is a particular concern in customer-facing businesses such as restaurants and retail stores. An additional factor is that a pandemic alters customer demand levels. For example, a pedicure operation might see its demand vanish overnight, while a manufacturer of surgical masks might experience a massive increase in demand.

The development of a pandemic management plan requires input from the human resources department, facilities management, union representatives, and (if there is no in-house expertise) a health care advisor. It may also be necessary to consult with the firm's most critical suppliers. This group oversees most activities involving person-to-person interactions, and so can provide the best input into how the business should be configured to deal with a pandemic.

The main focus of the plan should be on supporting the core functions of the business without being able to maintain a significant number of employees on the premises. This may result in recommendations to move more IT functions into the cloud, so that the firm is not directly responsible for the maintenance of computer hardware and software. Another likely outcome is recommendations to encourage employees to work from home, even in the absence of a pandemic, so that they can become comfortable with this arrangement, and to work out any bugs in the process before work-from-home arrangements are actually needed. Video conferencing can be used as a replacement for in-person meetings. Yet another possibility is to alter the work layout so that employees are situated further apart; this is a particular problem in work environments, such as production lines, where employees stand right next to each other for prolonged periods of time.

> **Tip:** Review customer contracts to see if the firm is subject to penalty clauses if deliveries are not made on time. As these contracts come up for renewal, try to adjust the penalty clauses to give the firm an out due to pandemic disruptions.

Sanitation becomes a significant concern in a pandemic. It may be necessary to clean commonly-used surfaces frequently, such as elevator buttons, vending machine buttons, light switches, and door handles. This can be a real problem in customer-facing environments, where there may be concerns about handling customer credit cards or signing documents with pens that are used by many people.

It may be necessary to revise the company sick policy during a pandemic. The key point is to encourage employees to stay home if they are sick. So, if the existing sick policy states that employees only get five days of sick time per year, they can be expected to return to work even when they are still sick, thereby infecting more employees. A better approach is to remove the cap on sick days for the duration of a pandemic, giving employees no reason to come into the office while they are still sick.

Another concern is who fills in for a sick person during a pandemic. There should be a designated backup for every key position, with a training plan for each of these backups. If preparatory training was not conducted prior to the declaration of a pandemic, then it should be conducted as soon thereafter as possible.

The plan should also mandate the immediate imposition of a policy to limit employee travel. Instead, they are encouraged to communicate with other parties via video chat or phone calls. When it is absolutely essential to travel, employees should be quarantined at home for a few days upon their return, to see if they have become infected.

The form of interaction with customers may have to change. At a minimum, Plexiglas barriers will probably need to be constructed. Other possibilities are requirements for physical separation, such as having everyone in a bank line stand at least six feet apart. Personal protective equipment, such as masks and gloves, may be required. Hand sanitizers should be made available to both employees and customers.

> **Tip:** As a preventive measure, obtain significant stocks of personal protective equipment and hand sanitizer, since these items will be in short supply as soon as a pandemic is declared by the health authorities.

A concern is the availability of raw materials. If borders are closed, can raw materials still be delivered from other countries? Or, a pandemic may hit a supplier's location so hard that it is unable to make deliveries, even if the borders remain open. For these reasons, it may be necessary to develop alternative sources of supply closer to home that can be called upon in the event of a pandemic.

A major concern to address as part of pandemic planning is whether the company is projected to be severely negatively impacted – and if so, what to do about it. For example, the government may shut down all bars and restaurants to limit disease transmission. Or, travel declines precipitously because no one wants to do so, resulting in drastic declines in business for airlines, hotels, and car rental agencies. Should management make alterations to the business model to guard against these risks? For example, hotels might promote the use of their conference room facilities for local businesses, while restaurants could expand their home delivery and takeout services. In other cases, management might accept the risk and instead cut back on debt levels in order to be in a better financial position when a pandemic occurs.

An essential element of pandemic management is continual communications with employees. This involves giving them the latest updates about safety procedures adopted by the company, policies for physical distancing, how and when to wear masks, whether they can work from home, and so forth. The firm might also want to communicate sickness policies, such as requiring employees to stay at home for a certain period of time if anyone in their household becomes sick. These communications are especially important at the start of a pandemic, when there is likely to be a great deal of uncertainty about what to do.

A final communications issue is to keep warning employees to keep their guard up until the health authorities declare that a pandemic is over. This can be difficult, especially as infection rates begin to decline and people become weary of complying with stay-at-home and social distancing directives.

Plan Updates

If the project team issues individual page updates to everyone holding copies of the disaster recovery plan, it is quite likely that some of the updates will not be inserted into the binder, making for inconsistent documentation across the organization. A more expensive but lower-risk approach is to swap out old binders with new ones, thereby ensuring that everyone authorized to have a plan is holding the most recent version.

Tip: Consider issuing the plan on encrypted USB flash drives, and encouraging the recipients to keep these drives readily at hand, such as in a purse or attached to a key chain.

Summary

When developing a disaster recovery plan, keep in mind that it must be as brief and easy-to-read as possible, because people will be relying on it during a time of great stress; if it is not easy to understand, they will ignore it.

Another essential point is that the plan is constantly changing. The first draft will be modified (perhaps extensively) once a round of testing has been completed, and will periodically require additional updates when there are process changes. Consequently, one must be mindful of the need for routine updates that are disseminated to key people within the company on a regular basis. This is especially necessary for technical recovery plans, which are so detailed that they will likely require frequent updates to keep current.

In addition, be sure to pay attention to the work area recovery plan. Many organizations focus excessively on recovering their IT functions, and minimize the recovery needs of the rest of the company. Since these other areas are supporting customers and are also less well protected from disasters than the IT department, it is well worthwhile to develop robust work area recovery plans.

Chapter 7
Crisis Management

Introduction

A system for crisis management is needed to deal with the first moments of a disaster. A standardized approach to the initial handling of a crisis can greatly mitigate losses and allow a firm to return to normal operations sooner. In this chapter, we cover the first steps needed to deal with a problematic situation, with a particular focus on the actions required by senior management and the emergency operations staff.

Initial Communications

Senior management is responsible for the initial decision regarding whether a disaster has occurred. If so, they trigger the disaster recovery plan by contacting those responsible for it. This initial contact is a weak point in the recovery process, since many people may need to be contacted within a short period of time. A good way to hasten this process is to use an autodialer to both call and text the emergency response teams.

If the initial indication is that a "disaster" is actually fairly limited in scope, management can hold off on the communications just described, and instead send one person in to evaluate the issue. If the on-site person finds that the issue is more extensive, then management can trigger the autodialer for a more broad-based response. This two-step approach can keep a number of crisis response people from being repeatedly called in for lesser emergencies.

Once the disaster recovery plan has been activated, senior management is responsible for supporting all phases of the recovery, which is mostly oriented toward providing the recovery teams with all the support needed to achieve the restoration of minimum acceptable service levels. In addition, management is ultimately responsible for all external communications. Also, if a business is publicly-held, they will need to keep the board of directors informed of the situation.

Crisis Management Best Practices

The exact nature of the steps taken during the early moments of a disaster will vary depending on the nature of the emergency, so instead of providing a standard list of actions to take, we list the following best practices that can be applied to most situations:

- *Call customers.* Key customers will be concerned about whether they can rely upon the company to meet its delivery commitments. Accordingly, call them as soon as possible to relay the latest status updates. In addition, consider acquiring the needed goods on the open market and transferring them to customers (even at a loss) just to make sure that all commitments are fulfilled.

- *Call legal counsel.* A disaster can trigger all sorts of lawsuits, such as for delays in delivering to customers or when an employee is killed. To head off these liabilities, one of the first steps in a crisis is to contact the company's legal counsel. This person can also be quite useful in negotiating with the firm's insurers over insurance settlement payments to be made to the business.
- *Call public relations.* If the company employs an outside public relations firm or has its own in-house staff, a lead person should be notified of the disaster as soon as possible, so that they can formulate a response to media questions. It can be useful for these parties to develop boilerplate press releases for different types of emergencies. Also, all emergency responders should be warned that they are not to talk to the press – that right is reserved for authorized public relations personnel.
- *Communicate about benefits.* When employees have been injured or killed, the human resources department should contact them or their families to discuss all available benefits, such as medical insurance and life insurance.
- *Communicate by text.* Communicating by text message is a good way to contact team members, because these messages require very little bandwidth, and so can get through an overburdened data network when voice calls are being dropped. An automated texting platform can send a standard message to a number of team members automatically, which frees up management time for other activities. The platform can also report back on who has been reached, which allows managers to shift to a backup person where needed. A related best practice is to periodically send out a text message, which validates whether the intended phone numbers are still being monitored.
- *Document injuries and fatalities.* When employees or outsiders are injured or killed, the human resources department needs to investigate and document the situation and send its findings to the firm's legal counsel. The documentation should include the time, place, and suspected cause of each incident.
- *Hire extra security.* When a facility is damaged, there is a risk that unauthorized people will enter it and make off with assets and confidential documents. Since the emergency response teams will likely be overwhelmed with other responsibilities, the best way to mitigate this loss may be to have a private security company send in a team to block access and ensure that everyone entering the facility is an authorized employee.
- *Preposition emergency supplies.* There are several standard supplies that can be used to recover from a variety of disasters. Examples of these supplies are tarps (to cover a damaged roof), flashlights and batteries (when the power is out) and wet vacuums (to suck out excess water).
- *Pull in off-site employees.* When a company has multiple subsidiaries, it may have people with duplicate skills in other facilities. If so, contact those whose skills can be used at the disaster site and get them on the next plane to the stricken area.
- *Remove salvageable items.* All assets and records that can be salvaged should be removed from the premises as soon as possible. This can be a problem

when insurance adjustors want to view these items in place first; if so, protect them as well as can be managed on-site, and then move them after the adjustors are through.

- *Shut off services*. The emergency teams should know exactly where the water, electrical, and gas shutoffs for the building are located, so that they can be turned off to mitigate damage. This is a particular concern for water mains, since flooding can cause irreparable damage.
- *Standardize team assembly points*. Identify one location within or adjacent to the facility where all members of the emergency response team are expected to meet once an emergency is declared. Doing so eliminates the uncertainty associated with where the other members of the team are located. An outside assembly point is generally better, since it addresses situations in which there is damage to the building.

Though most of the preceding best practices do not require the on-site presence of senior managers, they should still visit the site, in order to gain an understanding of what the company is facing and what it will take to remediate the situation.

The Emergency Operations Center

A disaster recovery plan should be coordinated from an emergency operations center. As the name implies, this is the location from which all containment and recovery operations are coordinated. The disaster containment manager is located here, and is tasked with collecting information from disaster sites and applying resources as needed to mitigate the damage and return to a level of minimum acceptable operations. This person will probably have to make on-the-fly adjustments to the disaster recovery plan, since the nature of the emergency and the exact situation in which it arises may not dovetail perfectly with the plan.

An emergency operations center is needed to achieve the highest level of efficiency possible. By coordinating resources from one central location, management can reduce the number of instances in which emergency teams are working at cross-purposes, so that everyone is working towards the same goal.

The ideal situation for an emergency operations center is being able to track the status of everyone who can potentially be assigned to a team, where they are located, the status of each recovery effort, when people will be relieved for downtime, and the projected times by which minimum services can be restored. This level of data gathering is ideal for the coordination of media messaging, since it centralizes recovery status information in one place.

> **Tip:** For an emergency operations center to function properly, pre-configure a location with all necessary technology and power backups, and make sure that all emergency personnel know how to access it.

If the company does not have sufficient funding to construct and maintain a permanent emergency operations center, then use the existing security office as a substitute. The security office is already set up with a radio base station, and so represents a reasonable alternative. To make this option work, consider expanding the security office, so that it can accommodate additional personnel during a crisis. Another option is to use a computer training room. These rooms are already configured with computers, and only need to have data and phone lines run in to make them reasonably operational. In either case, be sure to pre-position supplies for the operations center in a nearly supply room, so that supplies can be pulled out and positioned on short notice.

Another possibility for an emergency operations center is a mobile trailer that is outfitted with the necessary office equipment, satellite uplinks, emergency generator, and phones. It should be equipped with a large tent, in case operations expand outside of the trailer. It can be moved to wherever a disaster has been experienced. This is a good option when a company has a number of locations, so that the trailer can be shifted to wherever the emergency happens to be.

> **Tip:** Designate an extra emergency operations center, in case the first center is destroyed by whatever disaster impacted the company. This should be in a more distant location, in case a regional disaster – such as an earthquake – strikes. Though this secondary location may not be preconfigured with as many resources, at least ensure that there are enough data and phone lines running into it, so that it can achieve basic functionality in short order.

Emergency Operations Staffing

Everyone who will work in the emergency operations center should be identified well in advance and run through a variety of drills. By doing so, they will have a good understanding of their areas of responsibility during a disaster, and so will know where to go, what equipment to use, and which tasks to perform. To be safe, it makes sense to have a designated backup for each of these positions. Doing so not only covers for people who are away during a disaster, but also provides a second shift to relieve the primary crew.

The disaster containment manager is responsible for all decisions made in the operations center. Those decisions include:

- Activating emergency teams
- Assigning specific tasks to team members
- Approving equipment and material purchases
- Obtaining additional staffing as needed
- Declaring rest periods

Senior management should be quite clear about this person's level of authority, so that no department managers can walk in and override his or her decisions. To prevent these override issues, the disaster containment manager is usually someone sufficiently high up in the corporate hierarchy that few people would be in a position to contest his or her decisions. This manager must have sufficient time available to become acquainted with the firm's disaster recovery plan, as well as to participate in periodic training drills.

Emergency Operations Work Allocation

There are two teams working within the emergency operations center, where one team is focused on containment efforts and the other on restoring business operations to the minimum acceptable level. Most of the resources are initially allocated to the containment team, and are then gradually shifted to the recovery group as restoration efforts are completed.

The members of the containment team are called into the operations center first, and are responsible for coordinating all activities that minimize the damage to company facilities. Examples of these activities are establishing a secure perimeter around the impacted location, pumping out water, putting out fires, and plugging roof holes. This team is also responsible for safeguarding assets, both in terms of keeping them from being damaged further, and also to prevent them from being stolen. Once the initial containment efforts have been completed, the team will also need to sort through the wreckage to create an inventory of the remaining assets, their condition, and what it will take to restore them to workable condition.

The members of the recovery team will initially work with the company's insurance adjustors, who will want to see assets in place in order to make valid damage assessments. The recovery team can assist by documenting the location and condition of each damaged asset, and taking photographs to substantiate the documentation. This is an essential task, since the company needs to be paid by the insurer in order to fund the recovery effort.

Once the damage assessment is complete, the recovery team develops a plan for how to restore functionality and selectively adds team members to deal with the issues found. It is quite likely that the team will need representatives from the finance department to coordinate the transfers of cash needed to make repairs. In addition, one or more purchasing people will be needed to coordinate the acquisition of the necessary materials and equipment. Also, an accountant will need to keep track of all expenditures, so that the total cost of the recovery can be determined. A public relations coordinator will be needed for larger disasters, to develop all official announcements made by the company as they pertain to the disaster. Public relations is an especially important position when people have been killed or injured. A human resources person will be needed to call in employees for emergency assistance, as well as to deal with those who refuse to provide assistance. It is quite likely that the sales manager will also be needed, to deal with any customers who are concerned about the company's ability to ship goods to them in a timely manner. And of course, several members of the recovery team must have expertise in facility reconstruction.

Emergency Operations Preparation

A number of actions can be taken in advance to prepare an emergency operations center, to make it as functional as possible when a disaster strikes. The following bullet points contain many of the essentials that should be provided:

- *Communications*. Though everyone probably has a cell phone, one should also have radios on hand, as well as land lines, Internet connections, and televisions (for access to the news).
- *Medical supplies*. Keep an abundance of medical supplies on-site, on the assumption that a number of injuries will need to be treated.
- *Office supplies*. Lay in a stock of office supplies, such as copiers, computers, paper, and toner cartridges; disasters can create vast amounts of paperwork.
- *Power*. Install a backup generator and a battery backup. Their capacity should be based on the amount of equipment expected to be installed in the center. Be generous in settling upon the best capacity level to acquire. The generator should have sufficient fuel to run for an extended period of time.
- *Sanitary facilities*. Have sanitary facilities available nearby. Assume that water pressure will be lost at some point, which means that portable toilets will be needed.
- *Status boards*. Acquire several large white boards, on which the latest status information is posted. This is a good, centralized way to share information, such as containment and recovery status, current and upcoming activities, and who is currently on duty.

> **Tip:** Only allow one person to update the status boards, which minimizes the amount of unnecessary or inaccurate information that may be posted.

Emergency Operations Communications

The emergency operations center will receive a flood of information from the emergency teams and other parties. The staff can reasonably expect to receive team status reports, where employees are currently working, requests for equipment and materials, status reports on when those items will arrive, injury reports, inquiries from local emergency services, and inquiries from the news media. In addition, the staff will initiate a number of outbound communications, including calls to suppliers, customers, the news media, and senior management. Given the volume of calls going in and out, the center should be configured with an adequate number of phone lines and Internet connections.

Summary

Proper crisis management requires the management team to make an immediate assessment about the extent of the damage. They use this information to determine whether a full-blown disaster should be declared, or whether a more limited response is sufficient. In the former case, a number of best practices can be employed, either in advance or after a disaster is declared, to mitigate the damage. During this period, the emergency operations staff is responsible for communicating with outside parties and organizing resources to assist the recovery effort. Doing so enhances the efficiency of the containment and recovery efforts, which reduces costs and increases the speed with which a recovery can be made.

Chapter 8
Plan Testing

Introduction

A disaster recovery plan is not a proven, reliable tool until it has been tested – and on an ongoing basis. Until testing has occurred, a plan is merely a set of procedures that may or may not work. This task is essential, because plans that have been tested have a higher probability of success; these plans have been adjusted for problems found in the field. In this chapter, we discuss the advantages of and problems with plan testing, the types of tests that may be conducted, and testing strategy.

The Advantages of Plan Testing

Though the testing process can be a pain (as we will get into shortly), it results in a number of benefits for a business. Consider the following advantages:

- *Estimate recovery time.* A test can provide a reasonable estimate of how long it will take to recover from a disaster; deriving this estimate merely by poring over recovery procedures is a poor substitute.
- *Estimate resource requirements.* Only by testing a recovery plan can management obtain a reasonable estimate of the amount of resources to assign to a recovery effort.
- *Provide training.* Conducting a recovery test is an excellent way to provide training, because the people responsible for recovery tasks will be using the plan to conduct a simulated recovery. Doing so as a test eliminates many of the fumbles that will occur when a real disaster strikes.
- *Spot errors.* The process flow stated in a recovery plan may be incorrect or stated in a misleading manner. Only by walking through the plan during a test can one spot these issues.
- *Spot missing steps.* The first iteration of a recovery plan may be missing several steps. The missing steps are probably not apparent to someone writing the plan at a desk, and can only be discovered in the field. For example, the first draft of an IT recovery plan may not include where the passwords are located to unlock a server.
- *Spot update changes.* A recovery plan is only current as of the date when it is written. After that date, ongoing changes to processes will gradually render the plan invalid. For example, the replacement of a machine on the shop floor will require a new procedure for how to restart it after a power failure.

In short, testing a disaster recovery plan – not once, but on a recurring basis – results in a number of benefits that can be of great assistance when an actual disaster occurs.

The Difficulties of Plan Testing

It can be quite difficult to conduct plan testing. The specialists assigned to actually implement the plan during a real disaster must be made available to participate in the test. It can be exceedingly difficult to free up all of these people at the same time. In addition, some tests should be conducted in the locations and using the equipment that would be used during an actual disaster. This can be expensive, if the locations have to be rented. Or, if the intent is to move into space currently occupied by other operational areas, then conducting a test can be a major inconvenience for the displaced parties. And overlying all of these problems is resistance from department managers, who do not want to lose key staff for testing exercises. The result is likely to be excessively infrequent tests, with a tendency toward verbal walk-throughs that are not as effective as full-scale disaster simulations.

Types of Tests

A disaster recovery plan can be tested in a variety of ways, depending on the time and resources available for testing and the quality of the results produced. In increasing order of complexity, the following tests may be employed:

1. *Group review.* In this test, the person who wrote the plan reviews it with one or more people. Typically, those involved are from the disaster recovery planning team, and so have similar levels of expertise. This is a simple walkthrough, and is most useful for spotting errors and omissions.
2. *Verbal walk-through.* In this test, everyone assigned to enact the plan talks through the actions they will take as they methodically work their way through the planning document. Given the larger number of people involved, and with a broader range of backgrounds, it is likely that additional errors and omissions will be found.
3. *Incident response.* In this test, those charged with plan implementation are presented with a disaster scenario and asked to conduct a verbal walk-through of what they would do. Additional problems may be added during the discussion to test how the group responds. This test is usually held in a conference room, so no equipment is needed. It typically runs for two to four hours.
4. *Disaster simulation.* This test is similar to the incident response, except that the team is expected to work at the actual recovery site. This is the most realistic scenario, but also the most expensive one. It can be quite disruptive to company operations, and so is usually planned for a weekend or a slow time of the year. It may last for several days.

Of the four preceding tests, only a disaster simulation requires a substantial expenditure of time and expense. The other three can be conducted in a conference room within a relatively short period of time.

Tip: When conducting an incident response test or disaster simulation, have someone take notes about the series of decisions made. The notes should include what decisions were made, who made them, and when this was done. This information can be analyzed later to improve the disaster recovery plan.

The scenarios used for an incident response or disaster simulation should focus on the types of problems that a functional area is most likely to face. This could be a server crash in the IT department, a major machine malfunction in the manufacturing department, or the collapse of shelving in the warehouse. The scenarios selected should come from the project team's risk analysis, which lays out the types of issues that may arise. The following exhibit contains a number of possible scenarios for which tests could be constructed.

Possible Testing Scenarios

Broken water pipe	Explosion	Power failure
Chemical spill	Fire	Roof collapse
Civil unrest	Flood	Sabotage
Computer virus	Hurricane	Snowstorm
Data communications failure	Labor strike	Supply chain disruption
Earthquake	Landslide	Tornado
Equipment failure	Pandemic	Workplace violence

Tip: Use company events as an excuse for a disaster simulation. For example, when power is cut off for routine maintenance, follow the associated plan to see how well it works in turning power back on in the affected area. Or, when the company is planning to move to a new facility, set up a disaster simulation to coincide with the move, so that the firm's ability to switch to a backup facility can be evaluated.

The scenarios used in testing can employ real-world elements, such as incorrect information that is later adjusted, missing employees who are later found (or not), and initial damage assessments that are too high or too low. These elements are useful for testing how well employees deal with a chaotic situation.

Consider adding more information to a scenario as it progresses. For example, an initial report of workplace violence in the warehouse is later expanded, as a rogue employee goes on a shooting spree throughout the facility. Or, an initial report of tornado damage is later expanded to state that gas lines have ruptured because of the tornado, which has triggered explosions in the warehouse, which in turn have caused hazardous chemicals stored in the warehouse to leak.

EXAMPLE

The author once worked at the Jolly Rancher Candies production facility in Wheatridge, Colorado (which has since been moved). An employee was fired for cause, and returned to the company in a rage a few hours later with a pistol, with which he fired six shots into the sugar silo outside of the facility. This silo fed sugar directly into the company's candy production lines, so production had to be stopped until filters could be inserted into the sugar feed. It would be safe to say that this was an outlier risk for which the facility was not prepared!

Tip: Be sure to rove through a range of testing scenarios over time, rather than repeating the same ones. Otherwise, employees will get bored with them and try to escape from this assignment.

Scenarios may be applied in layers to more realistically simulate a disaster. For example, a scenario on a cruise ship begins with a small fire on the bridge, which is eliminated when the water sprinkler system is activated – which in turn damages the controls for the rudder, making the ship more difficult to turn. Scenarios can also be designated to occur at night, on weekends, or during a holiday, in order to test whether the few staff still on site can respond adequately and call in emergency personnel in a timely manner.

In addition to the preceding sequence of tests, the IT staff may conduct a series of IT recovery tests. These tests work under the assumption that a system is entirely nonoperational and needs to be brought back up to working condition. For example, a test might conduct a cold start of the accounting software, the email server, or the company network. These tests are also useful for spotting the interfaces with other systems that must be operational before a system will operate properly. For example, recovering the accounting system may require that the purchasing and warehouse management systems be operational first, so that the accounting system can access records stored in those two systems.

Tip: A good place to perform IT recovery tests is at the company's IT recovery hot site. Doing so gives management a good idea of the amount of recovery time that will actually be required when dealing with the same type of disaster.

When an actual incident arises and has been dealt with, the emergency management teams should meet within a few days to conduct an after-action review. The intent of this review is to discuss what worked and where there are opportunities for improvement. However, if this meeting is held after more than a few days have passed, then memories of the event will have clouded, resulting in a less informational meeting.

EXAMPLE

There is a fire at Monk Books, which makes presentation-grade copies of medieval books. During the after-action meeting, it was noted that the alarms worked fine and everyone evacuated safely, but that only half of the fire suppression system functioned properly, and the batteries in the emergency lights did not function. Decisions made were to schedule a maintenance check of the fire suppression system and to swap out the batteries in the emergency lights. In addition, the activities calendar now includes a quarterly check of both issues.

The Testing Strategy

A testing strategy is needed to maximize the benefits from testing a disaster recovery plan. The strategy lays out the types and frequency of tests that will be conducted. Based on this strategy, one should create a testing calendar that runs several years into the future, so that the time of participants can be blocked out well in advance. The schedule will have to be structured around the seasonal activities of the various departments, which may be much busier in some months than in others.

> **Tip:** Obtain written approval from senior management for the testing strategy, as well as their active support. This is critical, since department managers will resist having their people taken away for testing activities.

The testing strategy is based on the business impact analysis, which was described earlier in this book. When the analysis states that the recovery time objective must be short, then the testing strategy must mandate both comprehensive and frequent testing. When the recovery time objective is longer, a more relaxed strategy can be adopted.

Even in companies where the recovery time can be relatively long, there will probably be a few niche operations where the recovery time must be substantially shorter. For these operations, the strategy should mandate more thorough and frequent testing. For example, an Internet store will probably need to focus its strategy on recovering the server that hosts the website.

It is generally not possible to shut down company operations and conduct a comprehensive disaster recovery test, since it interferes too much with ongoing business operations. Instead, the testing strategy focuses on a rolling examination of different parts of the business. Thus, a test might address issues in the warehouse in January, the finance department in March, and the engineering department in May. A variation is to test a group of related business processes. Depending on the business impact analysis for each of these areas, it might be sufficient to conduct a verbal walk-through in the finance and engineering departments, and an incident response in the warehouse. IT tests may need to be conducted on a quarterly basis, while pandemic tests are addressed only once a year. The mix selected will depend on the issues identified in the business impact analysis.

Summary

The testing process is not designed to force employees into making "right" choices. Instead, it is intended to clarify and improve upon existing plans, while keeping them flexible enough to deal with a variety of situations. To ensure that this happens, management should support an ongoing series of tests that encompass all areas for which there is a disaster recovery plan. Most of these tests are likely to be short walk-throughs in a conference room, but a few disaster simulations should be planned in order to review the ability of the company to recover in areas where a short recovery time is mandated.

Chapter 9
Policy Adjustments

Introduction

A business has probably installed a set of policies that guide how it conducts operations. These policies are intended to put guardrails around the boundaries of acceptable behavior, ensure that certain operations are properly controlled, and keep operations running within the boundaries of all applicable laws and regulations. What they are *not* designed to do is provide assistance when a disaster strikes. In this chapter, we cover the policies that require adjustment in order to maintain operations during a crisis.

Employee Assistance Program Policy

An employee assistance program is a work-based intervention program that is intended to assist employees in resolving personal problems that could impact their performance. These programs assist employees with alcohol or substance abuse, as well as financial and legal problems, wellness, and traumatic events.

The policy covering an employee assistance program should state that employees be notified of the program's features immediately following a disaster, especially in regard to assistance with handling traumatic events. A high level of participation in the program is encouraged, so that employees can return to normal as soon as possible. The policy can encourage supervisors to recommend the program to those employees whose mental state has been adversely affected by a disaster.

Employee Attendance Policy

When an organization requires employees to work from the office, it probably has an attendance policy. This policy states the normal operating hours during which employees are expected to be on the premises, and the penalties for being late.

During a disaster, the last thing the employer wants to do is to encourage people to come to the office. When a company facility is flooded or on fire – and especially during a pandemic – employees need to stay home. To encourage them to not come in, the attendance policy should be modified to state the conditions under which employees should stay home, and note that they will not be penalized for doing so.

An additional enhancement to the attendance policy is to allow flexible working hours and no dress code at all during the recovery period following a disaster. By doing so, employees can attend to any cleanup issues at home (such as cleaning up after a hurricane has passed through), while still making it into the office when it is possible to do so.

Off-Hours Access Policy

Some businesses have a policy that restricts employees from gaining access to company facilities during hours outside of the firm's normal operating hours. This policy is most common when an organization stores confidential information or expensive assets that can be stolen.

During a disaster, emergency teams may be accessing the facility at all hours of the day or night. In addition, other employees need to work late to catch up on the work they missed during the period covered by the disaster. Further, the emergency teams may have forced access by breaking open doors that were normally intended to be locked. In short, the access situation is entirely different both during and after a disaster. Given these circumstances, the access policy should be expanded to state who is permitted to authorize emergency access to the facility, who maintains the list of people who are granted emergency access, and the types of identification documents they must produce when being reviewed for access. Also, for information and asset protection purposes, the policy may state special access authorizations for certain parts of the facility.

Payroll Policy

The standard company payroll policy typically states the procedures to be followed to pay hourly workers, such as a requirement to clock in and out, with approval requirements for overtime hours worked. If employees do not work, then they are not paid. This is a major problem in a disaster, where company facilities are closed and employees cannot work.

The payroll policy should address workarounds to these problems. For example, it might state that employees will be paid if the company is shut down due to a disaster, or that alternative timekeeping arrangements will be employed, or that all employees are assumed to have worked a 40-hour week if the clock-in system is not accessible.

> **Tip:** Install a procedure to pay employees based on the most recent pay period if the payroll system is currently not operational due to a disaster, after which the difference will be calculated from actual hours worked and adjusted in the following pay period.

Purchasing Policy

The corporate purchasing policy usually outlines a regimented process for what types and amounts of expenditures must be approved by managers – sometimes involving a series of approvals for larger purchases. This policy is intended to maintain tight control over expenditures.

The purchasing policy should be adjusted to reflect the reality of a disaster recovery, where large amounts have to be spent immediately in certain areas to ensure that a company can recover as quickly as possible. To make this possible, the policy should state which categories of purchases can be made without approval during a disaster, what constitutes a disaster, and the preferred suppliers for these purchases. Also, since these purchases may involve the use of personal or corporate credit cards, the policy should outline how to properly document the purchases.

Sick Leave Policy

Most organizations have some type of sick leave policy, which states how much sick time a person earns per day, and the conditions under which it can be claimed. This policy is designed to put a cap on the amount of paid sick time that an employee is allowed to take, after which they are expected to be back in the office.

There are two circumstances in which the standard sick leave policy will not work in a disaster. First, employees may have been injured in the disaster, and so will not be able to return to work for some time. In this case, the policy could be waived entirely or a larger number of sick leave days may be allowed. Second – and more importantly – a sick leave policy is entirely counterproductive when there is a pandemic, since it encourages infected people with no remaining sick leave to come to the office, potentially infecting other employees. In this latter case, the policy should have no cap at all, so that employees are paid as long as they are sick. In addition, the policy should encourage them to stay home if a family member is sick, under the assumption that the employees have been or will become infected, too.

Social Media Policy

A business may have a social media policy that states guidelines for what types of information employees should be posting about the company on social media. This policy is intended to protect the firm's reputation. When there is a disaster, the policy may need to be more restrictive, since adverse comments about the condition of the business could impact the decisions of suppliers to continue selling to the company, as well as customers to buy from it. In short, the policy should state that information about the incident should only be made by authorized persons, including such issues as the amount of damage incurred and the amount of time it will take to recover from the situation.

Vacation Policy

The typical vacation policy states the amount of vacation time that an employee earns per day, and how it must be used (such as during the current year, or with a modest number of unused hours carrying over into the next year).

It may be necessary to expand upon these basic vacation policies to address *where* employees are going on vacation. For example, if they go to a region where there are known health risks from communicable diseases as identified by the Centers for Disease Control or the World Health Organization, then they will be required to work from home for a certain number of days before being allowed back into the office. A more aggressive policy would be to strongly advise employees not to vacation in these areas, and possibly even restrict them from doing so. Another possibility is to formally state that the company has the right to cut short the vacations of those employees considered critical to disaster recovery efforts and fly them back at company expense in order to assist with such activities.

Work-from-Home Policy

A business might have a policy that restricts who can work from home, and for how long. The policy is designed to keep people in the office, such as by requiring special permission to work from home, and even then, only for a certain number of consecutive days – perhaps due to a person taking maternity leave.

In a disaster, it may be impossible to come to the office, so this policy should be eliminated. The reverse policy may be needed, such as giving high priority to setting up employees at home with computer access to the company's systems. The policy could mandate that the IT department give a high priority to visiting employee homes to set up virtual private network links into the company network, and to ensure that employees know how to access the system. In addition to these initial set-up arrangements, the work-from-home policy should address the following additional points:

- How to handle confidential information at home
- Whether there are any mandatory time periods when employees must be working on company business
- The range of hours over which employees are expected to work

Summary

A company's policies need to be fine-tuned to address the realities of a disaster, so that employee actions are in alignment with the needs of the business at that time. This means encouraging employees to stay away from work when they are sick, spend money quickly to recover company operations, work from home when the office is damaged, and so forth. The required policy adjustments should be made now, not after a disaster has already occurred, so that the firm is not hamstrung by counterproductive policies.

Chapter 10
Disaster-Related Best Practices

Introduction

There are a number of specific actions that a business can take to mitigate its risks in relation to certain types of disasters. In this chapter, we describe an array of activities that can collectively result in a much-reduced risk profile for a business. The actions to be taken cover a firm's business partners, as well as business records, computer workstations, electricity, fire mitigation, human resources, information, safety, telecommunications, and terrorism.

Business Partners

A disaster at a supplier may have a significant impact on a business, as would a disaster at the firm's customers. In this section, we address how to deal with customers and suppliers when disasters strike.

Customers

Customers do not appreciate it when a supplier experiences a disaster and then does nothing to notify them. With no notice, customers have no time to make alternate plans, and may suffer crises of their own when goods and services do not arrive from the supplier when expected. The best workaround is to develop a notification plan, so that a team immediately assesses the impact of a disaster on customers, and notifies customers of the impact on them. The sales staff should be the ones to convey this information, since they already have established relationships with customers. When discussing the matter with customers, the sales staff should be fully informed about the following items:

1. Which customer orders are currently open;
2. Which products are already in transit to the customer;
3. Which products can be fulfilled from undamaged company warehouses; and
4. The amount of time required to fulfill all remaining items on order.

It is also useful to call customers when operations have been fully restored. This drives away any remaining customer uncertainty, and may stop them from searching for replacement suppliers.

If necessary, the sales staff can also offer to assist customers in acquiring replacement products from other sources. By taking these steps, customers will form a more positive opinion about how the company tried to help them, rather than obfuscating the facts about a bad situation. In short, when handled properly, a disaster can strengthen a firm's ties with its customers.

When implementing a customer notification plan, the following best practices can be applied:

- *Frequent customer list*. Run a year-end listing of which 20% of customers are buying 80% of its goods and services (the Pareto principle). This shortened customer list should be the main focus of the notification plan, since they comprise most of the organization's business.
- *Contact information*. Add to the frequent customer list the applicable customer contact information, as well as the name of the assigned salesperson. This information is essential for rolling out notifications.
- *Penalty clauses*. Review customer contracts to see which ones impose penalties for late deliveries. Note these penalties on the frequent customer list; these customers will need to be prioritized.

Tip: Ensure that the sales staff can access the frequent customer list from a mobile device, since a disaster may not allow them to come into the office to access it from a computer.

Suppliers

There are multiple scenarios in which suppliers cannot supply goods by the expected date. It might involve damage to their facility, or to the facility of one of *their* suppliers, or events occurring during the transport of goods from their facility to the company. There are many ways in which transported goods can be interrupted, such as a strike by a longshoremen's union blocking ocean freight deliveries, an ice storm shutting down highways, and bad weather interrupting air freight deliveries. These supplier-related issues are among the more common concerns for a business, and so might not even be classified as disasters, because they occur so frequently. Nonetheless, a set of best practices can be developed to assist in the planning for supplier problems. Consider implementing the following steps:

- *Critical suppliers*. Identify those suppliers whose products are essential to the company. Some of these suppliers may not be obvious. Review the industry news to understand the types of supplier problems that have impacted competitors. Keep in mind that a service provider may be classified as a critical supplier, such as the firm's Internet service provider.
- *Contact information*. Maintain an updated list of contacts for the most critical suppliers, as well as for the purchasing agents assigned to them.
- *Data links*. Set up data links into the inventory management systems of critical suppliers in order to see the status of the company's orders, as well as how much additional inventory the suppliers have in stock. This information is essential for determining the amounts of products that will need to be sourced elsewhere if these suppliers are shut down.
- *Disaster planning*. Contact the critical suppliers and discuss with them what they will do in the event of a disaster. Not only does this result in some useful

preliminary planning, but also highlights any suppliers who are not interested in developing plans – which targets them for replacement.

- *Alternate transport.* Discuss with suppliers a backup plan for deliveries. For example, if air traffic is blocked for whatever reason, identify the next-fastest mode of transport and who that carrier will be.
- *Alternate suppliers.* Create a list of alternates for the critical suppliers. A good source of this information is suppliers that the company has used in the past. In addition, consider setting up these alternates with a string of lower-volume purchase orders, so that the company will have an existing relationship with them when it asks for a sudden ramp-up in purchase volumes.
- *Reserve supplies.* Calculate the maximum amount of time for which key supplies are· likely to be interrupted, and build up an inventory buffer in that amount. This build-up will need to be balanced against the cost of holding the extra inventory.
- *Alternative product designs.* When there is only one supplier for a key part, it can make sense to revise the products into which that part is incorporated, in order to eliminate the company's reliance on that supplier. This is obviously a long-term solution; in the short term, the best approach may be to stockpile the applicable part as a safety buffer.

When conducting a supplier analysis, be aware that not all purchases are directed to the firm's production operations. It is quite possible that essential supplies are going to other departments as well, in which case the critical suppliers list should include them.

> **Note:** A possible outcome of a critical supplier analysis is that a company finds itself with fewer suppliers. This is because the most marginal ones have been eliminated in favor of concentrating purchases with those suppliers that have disaster recovery plans.

Business Records

An organization may not be able to recover from the loss of certain business records, such as title to assets, customer invoices, contracts, personnel files, and investment records. All of these records are needed to maintain operations. In addition, a company may be required to maintain additional records in order to comply with a variety of legal requirements, such as sales tax reporting and hazardous waste disposal forms. The concern from a disaster recovery planning perspective is to understand where these records are located, how to safeguard them, and how to restore them following a disaster event. The path followed will depend on the record in question, since some documents require different types of safeguarding, and will need to be restored more quickly.

The most immediate best practice for dealing with business records is to adopt a records retention policy. This policy states which records must be retained, and for how long. In addition, the policy states how and where records are to be retained, and how the containers in which they are stored are to be identified. By doing so, a business can destroy records on a regular schedule when they are no longer legally required or irrelevant to business operations. This ongoing records reduction concentrates one's attention on those records that actually *need* to be protected.

> **Tip:** Be sure to stringently follow the corporate records destruction policy. Doing so clears out records storage space, clarifying which records really need to be recovered following a disaster.

The first step in dealing with business records is to conduct an inventory of them. Itemize what they are, where they are located, and the type of media on which they are stored. A surprising outcome is just how widely spread these records are throughout the business, parked in closets, desk drawers, and storage boxes in the warehouse. Therefore, it is essential to know where records are located, so that they can be more expeditiously located following a disaster.

Another outcome of this analysis is the types of media on which records are stored. This is important from a records storage and restoration perspective, since some types of media respond poorly to particular types of damage. For example, a deep freeze can harm a hard drive but has little impact on paper records, while paper responds poorly to fire.

The next step is to prioritize which records are most critical to the ongoing survival of the business. Doing so allows for an analysis of which records need to be afforded the most in-depth protection, and which ones need to be recovered first. When assigning a criticality score to a record type, keep in mind the cost to reproduce records when the originals are destroyed. When the reproduction cost is high (usually because records must be recompiled from other sources) then they may require a higher score.

> **Tip:** Use a simple coding tag to designate the criticality level of various records. For example, a red sticker indicates that a box of records absolutely must be recovered. The simplicity of this approach makes it easy for emergency teams not trained in records management to spot and retrieve the most vital records.

Create a record storage system that protects the most critical records. For example, put essential documents in fire-proof safes. Or, when there are multi-shelf storage racks, put the most critical records on the middle shelves in order to protect them from water damage (on the bottom shelves) or sprinkler damage (on the top shelf). Mark these locations in the disaster recovery plan, so that recovery teams know precisely where to go to recover them.

> **Tip:** When there are no shelves in the storage area, store records on pallets. Doing so keeps them a few inches off the floor, thereby reducing the risk of water damage.

Some disasters relating to record storage occur over a long period of time, usually due to unacceptably large swings in the temperature and humidity levels that gradually destroy records. To prevent this, install humidity and temperature sensors to track these changes over time, to see when out-of-bounds conditions are occurring. Based on the resulting information, install heating and air conditioning systems that maintain humidity and temperature within recommended ranges for records storage. If magnetic media are also being stored, then install an air filtration system to minimize the number of particulates in the air.

Magnetic tapes require especially careful storage protocols, in addition to the temperature and humidity issues just noted. They should always be stored in protective containers and on end (not with the reels parallel to the shelf surface). Further, they should not be stored in direct sunlight, nor should they be kept anywhere near a magnetic field. If these measures are not taken, then the data stored on the tapes may be corrupted.

There are several risk mitigation steps that can be applied to records storage. One is to install smoke and fire detection systems in the storage locations, with alarms situated in the security area. In addition, consider installing a gas-based fire suppression system in the storage area, though it is expensive. A less expensive option is to be profligate in installing fire extinguishers throughout the storage area; make sure that employees know how to use them. A good fire-mitigation policy is to keep all trash out of the storage area, which extends to not having any trash receptacles there at all – trash is just a source of fuel in the event of a fire. A final risk mitigation measure is to minimize the use of electrical equipment in the storage area, which extends to a ban on the use of extension cords.

> **Tip:** When records are absolutely essential, make copies of them and store the copies off-site, preferably in a facility with protection levels similar to those just described.

A final issue relating to records storage is security. An unauthorized person could gain access to confidential company records, making copies of such matters as company plans, product designs, and customer credit card information. To prevent this, restrict access to records storage, either with a door look or an electronic lock that keeps track of exactly who entered the storage area.

Several procedures can also be applied to the records storage area. For example, security guards can be asked to inspect the area for water damage every day, while also ensuring that all access points have been properly locked. At longer intervals, such as quarterly, an action checklist can mandate that all alarms be tested, fire extinguishers inspected, and air filters swapped out. In addition, conduct a periodic inspection for pests, which may lead to a call to a pest control outfit. These simple procedures can catch problems before records are damaged.

Another part of the storage plan is to regularly shift records to offsite storage. This is most easily arranged for digital records by using automated cloud storage, where records are saved to an offsite location in the background, without any actions being taken by employees. If tape backups are still used, then multiple copies should be stored offsite, and possibly in different locations. Tapes should only be shipped when temperatures are cool, to avoid heat damage. Finally, paper records not needed for ongoing operations should be shifted to off-site storage, if only because the storage cost will be cheaper. Offsite storage should be in a high-security location, with good environmental controls and fire suppression systems.

> **Tip:** When shipping records to offsite storage via third party carrier, require the carrier to obtain a signature from the receiving party. Doing so makes it easier to track down records that are lost in transit.

When a disaster occurs and after the fire department allows access to the building, the first step is to conduct a damage assessment, noting in particular the condition of those records tagged as being high priority. If there was a fire, verify that filing cabinets have cooled off before opening them. Once high-priority documents have been extracted, identify the level of damage they have sustained, and determine the recovery method to apply to each one. Send the most important documents out for immediate recovery work, and freeze lower-priority documents with dry ice for attention at a later date. Freezing a document can preserve it in its current state for as long as five years, and has the added benefits of reducing stain damage and eliminating mold.

The best way to rapidly recover documents is to contract in advance with a records recovery company, which comes onto the premises and immediately engages in recovery efforts. The usual process is air drying in a low-humidity environment, though books require more careful treatment involving freeze drying. It may be necessary to photocopy damaged documents (especially ones damaged by fire), and then use the photocopies instead of the originals.

The emphasis here is on recovery speed, rather than cost, since documents can be irreparably damaged within a short period of time. However, in the event of a general disaster, the contracted company may be overwhelmed with customer calls, and so may not be able to arrive right away.

As documents clear the recovery process, they will need to be stored in a new location that has adequate security, as well as humidity and temperature controls. This will require fast work to line up a replacement storage location, as it is likely that some documents were undamaged and so will need to be transferred there immediately.

There may be cases in which records were not damaged during a disaster. If so, ascertain whether air conditioning and heat can still be supplied to the storage area, and that it can be properly secured. If not, it may still be necessary to move the records to an offsite location, since the risk of future theft or damage may be too high. This is not a minor decision, since the effort required to move bulky records can be substantial.

Computer Workstations

The computer networks in most organizations are comprised of computer-based workstations sprinkled throughout the organization, rather than dumb terminals that merely access a central server. This presents a problem, because it means that crucial information is being stored all over the company, rather than in one place where it can be centrally managed. In addition, essential software may be stored on just one or two computers, so if those computers fail, the company has just lost some key functionality. Furthermore, given the dispersed nature of these devices, many are located in insecure places, which increases the odds of asset theft.

A number of best practices relating to disaster recovery planning for computer workstations are noted in the following bullet points:

- *Backup media*. Any type of file backup media used are not password protected, so be sure to store them in a locked location.
- *Computer replacements*. Create a schedule for ongoing computer replacements, so that equipment is swapped out before it can fail. The replacement schedule will vary with the equipment, but consider imposing a cap of no more than four years on all replacements. If a computer is positioned in an area with temperature and humidity extremes, then replace it more frequently.
- *Equipment locks*. Lock computers to desks with a steel cable. Doing so makes it much more difficult for anyone to make off with assets. A variation is to lock workstations in a ventilated cabinet, with just the keyboard and monitor positioned outside of the cabinet.
- *File backups*. It can be difficult to impose a backup regimen on everyone who operates a computer, so a reasonable alternative is to install a company-wide automated backup system that copies files to a third-party data storage site, using Internet connections. Another approach is to require employees to store all files identified as critical on the company's file server, so that a centralized backup plan can be applied to the files on the server. In some cases, this may mean that employees store *all* of their files on the file server.
- *File lists*. Create a list of just the key files stored on each computer – those that are critical to operations. Develop a backup plan for these files, and periodically verify that it is being followed.
- *Original software library*. Collect the CDs on which software was originally acquired and store it in a safe place. These CDs may be needed if computers crash or subsequent upgrades prove to be unstable.
- *Portable devices*. Given the increased risk of theft and damage associated with portable computers, they should be backed up prior to every business trip. Also, educate employees about the need to keep these devices out of sight during travel, to reduce the risk of theft.
- *Power protection*. Install a surge protector on the power line for every computer, to protect against power spikes. In addition, install a UPS on all desktop computers, since they do not have a built-in battery to protect against a loss of power.
- *Software license records*. The company may be subject to a software audit, so maintain a list of software licenses by workstation, to prove that all software copies were legitimately purchased.
- *Software lists*. Create a list of the key software used on each computer, so that it can be reloaded into a new computer if the existing computer crashes.

Electricity

The essential ingredient for most businesses is electricity. Without it, computer systems and most machinery are rendered inoperable. There are several ways to mitigate the risk of loss due to electricity problems. The simplest and least expensive is to install surge protectors on the electrical lines feeding into all powered equipment. Doing so eliminates equipment damage caused by power surges, which may arise from nearby lightning strikes, power transitions in large equipment on the same power line, or malfunctions caused by the power company. Surge protectors are typically built into power strips. The best surge protectors have a rating of at least 600 joules, which measures their ability to dissipate a power surge. Also, a quality surge protector should have a response time for blocking voltage spikes of ten nanoseconds or less.

> **Tip:** Surge suppressors do not last forever, so consider swapping them out on a regular replacement schedule, as per the manufacturer's recommendations.

Another protective device is a power conditioner. This acts as a buffer between the electrical outlet and company equipment, smoothing out voltage fluctuations that can impact system performance. There are several variations on the concept. A passive-type filter shunts high-frequency noise components away, through a capacitor or to ground; this is the most basic option. A balanced transformer produces better noise reduction, but is larger and heavier. The most expensive option is the AC regenerative-type conditioner, which uses automatic voltage stabilization circuitry to deliver the cleanest possible voltage to company equipment.

Another preventive measure is to install uninterruptible power supplies (UPS) on the electrical lines feeding into all powered equipment. This is essentially a large battery, which is frequently combined with a built-in surge protector. It allows equipment to continue running for a short time even after the main power source is not operating, so that the equipment can be shut down in an orderly manner. The size of the battery depends on the power usage of the equipment being supported and the amount of time that the UPS is expected to provide power. UPS batteries need to be replaced at regular intervals, so a replacement schedule should be followed based on the manufacturer's recommendations. Remote monitoring software can be used to check on the status of UPS batteries.

> **Tip:** Install a power conditioner between the power source and a UPS, since this reduces the load on the UPS batteries, thereby prolonging the battery life.

To keep a UPS running longer, a business should have a power shedding plan, where it shuts down non-essential equipment in order to reduce the battery drain, allowing the remaining equipment to be run from the UPS for a longer period of time. This power shedding plan should be a formal list that details exactly which equipment should be turned off. A simple way to identify non-essential equipment is to put a colored tag on each one that can be turned off; that way, someone can simply walk through a facility, spot the tags, and turn off the associated equipment.

A larger business may elect to pay for a backup power generator, or one which must have 24×7 access to power, such as a pharmaceuticals storage facility. This unit automatically starts up when there is a power loss and begins providing electricity to the facility. The interval between when power is lost and when the backup generator begins providing power is covered by an in-house UPS system. This is quite an expensive option, which must be set up with a substantial fuel reserve to power it for extended periods of time. This generator should be tested at regular intervals to ensure that it operates properly. Also, given its importance, the company must adhere to the manufacturer's recommended maintenance schedule.

> **Note:** Consider installing security features around the backup power generator, especially when immediate access to electricity is critical to the company. A sabotaged power generator could cause massive losses for a business in terms of downtime.

When power is lost, a company is required by law to have emergency lights installed around the facility. These lights are powered by batteries, which should be checked and replaced in accordance with the manufacturer's recommendations.

Fire Mitigation

One of the worst disasters a company can face is a fire, since it impacts the structural integrity of a building and absolutely destroys paper-based records. It also presents a high risk of fatality for employees. Given these concerns, consider implementing the following best practices to mitigate the risk of fires:

- *Additional sensors.* Install extra smoke detectors in parts of the facility that are normally unoccupied, where fires would have a better chance to grow undetected.
- *Alarm monitoring.* Either hire an outside service to monitor smoke sensors within the facility or have the security department do the monitoring.
- *Electrical inspections.* Have an electrician periodically tour the facility and make note of unsafe electrical issues, such as having too many appliances connected to a single electrical outlet. This should be an annual inspection, since the demand for electricity will change over time.
- *Evacuation practice.* Conduct periodic evacuation drills for the entire staff, to monitor how well the evaluation plan is working. Doing so also reduces the level of employee panic if there is a real emergency.
- *Evacuation review.* Examine the employee evacuation plan to see if it can be improved upon. There are many possible enhancements, including the use of evacuation supervisors to ensure that areas are clear, the posting of exit maps, assigning responsibility to shut down dangerous operations, and setting up outdoor assembly areas.
- *Extinguisher inspections.* Conduct a monthly review of all fire extinguishers on the premises to see if they are fully charged.

- *Extinguisher training*. Conduct training on the use of fire extinguishers with those employees most likely to use them. The basic sequence of events is to pull the pin, aim the outflow at the base of the flames, squeeze the trigger, and sweep the outflow from side to side.
- *Fire barriers*. Install fire doors and firewalls where needed to protect valuable assets, such as the computer room.
- *Fire inspections*. Hire a fire inspector to walk through the facility and point out fire risks. This should be an annual inspection, since ongoing office re-configurations present new fire risks.
- *Space heater policy*. Impose a policy that bans all space heaters from the premises. These heaters can cause fires, since they are a heat source.
- *Sprinkler inspections*. Conduct a periodic inspection of the sprinkler system. Items to look for are corroded pipes that could impede the flow of water, the reliability of the water source, and the condition of the sprinkler heads.
- *Timed electrical outlets*. Install a timer on an electrical outlet in the company kitchen, and plug the coffee machine into it. Doing so ensures that the machine is powered down during non-business hours.
- *Trash day*. Conduct a periodic tour of the facility and have employees clear out areas in which excess materials have piled up.

An additional best practice is to be profligate in installing fire extinguishers around the facility. However, the type of extinguisher used depends on the type of fire to which it is most likely to be applied. The following exhibit portrays the five classes of fires.

Five Classes of Fires

Class of Fire	Description
A	Freely-burning, combustible solid materials such as wood or paper
B	Flammable liquid or gas
C	Energized electrical fire (there is an electrical source)
D	Metallic fire (caused by titanium, zirconium, magnesium, or sodium)
K	Cooking fires, typically from animal or vegetable oils or fats

No matter which type of fire, there will always be four elements present, which are fuel, heat, oxygen, and a chain reaction. The theory behind the use of portable fire extinguishers is that a fire can be extinguished by removing one or more of these four elements.

For each class of fire, the fuel, heat source and chain reaction varies, which is why there are different types of fire extinguishers for each class of fire. Thus, while a Class A fire can be safely extinguished with water, this is not possible for a Class C fire, since water can conduct electricity and harm the operator of a fire extinguisher. Given these issues, there are six types of fire extinguishers that may be used, depending on the class of fire. They are as follows:

- *ABC powder fire extinguisher*. This is a multi-purpose fire extinguisher that sprays a chemical powder composed of monoammonium phosphate. The powder blankets and suffocates the fire. This type of extinguisher works on Class A, B, and C fires.
- *Carbon dioxide fire extinguisher*. This is one of the cleanest extinguishers, since it leaves no residue and requires no cleanup. It releases carbon dioxide, which removes oxygen from a fire, thereby suffocating it. This type of extinguisher works on Class B fires that involve flammable liquids, as well as electrical fires.
- *Wet chemical fire extinguisher*. This extinguisher is targeted at Class K fires. It uses a potassium solution to blanket a fire and creates a thick soap-like substance that seals the surface of the liquid that is on fire. It can also be used on Class A fires.
- *Water mist fire extinguisher*. This extinguisher works against most classes of fire. It sprays microscopic water molecules, which reduce the level of oxygen in the air while also cooling the fire. In addition, the water has been de-ionized so that it does not act as a conductor, which means that it can also be used on electrical fires. This combination of features makes it effective for use on Class A, B, C, and K fires.
- *Foam fire extinguisher*. This extinguisher sprays a foam that expands when it reaches the air and blankets a fire. This blanket prevents the vapors from rising off the liquid to feed a fire, thereby starving it of fuel. Also, since the foam is mixed with water, it has a cooling effect on the fire. This type of extinguisher works well on Class A fires and the flammable liquids of Class B fires.
- *Clean agent fire extinguisher*. This extinguisher sprays a gas, such as Halon, that extinguishes fire by reducing the oxygen level. This gas is non-conductive, leaves no residue, and is safe for use near people. This type of extinguisher is most commonly used on Class B and C fires.

Human Resources

When a disaster strikes a business, it can have a seriously negative impact on employees, since it interferes with their work and presents the possibility that their employer could go out of business. The human resources department can step in to deal with employee concerns in the midst of a disaster in order to enhance morale and keep people focused on returning to normal operations. Some of the best practices that the human resources department can employ to this end are noted in the following bullet points:

- *Adjusted work policies*. The department can modify the standard corporate work policies to conform to the realities of a crisis. An especially good one is allowing flexible work hours and working from home – essentially allowing employees to work whenever and wherever they can.

- *Debriefing.* In the midst of a crisis, it can be useful for the human resources staff to meet with groups of employees for a debriefing. The main point is to allow employees to bleed off some stress by talking them through the experience. The people who need these debriefs can be identified by walking around the facility and identifying those who appear to be impaired by the experience.

- *Direct assistance.* The department can set up temporary daycare facilities for the children of employees, so that the employees have an incentive to come to work. In addition, the department can set up emergency shelters for employees and their families, and provide meals to them.

- *Employee skills matrix.* The department should maintain a database that includes the key skills of every employee. These skills include having a working knowledge of key company processes. This is an asset during a disaster, when an employee may be injured or killed, and someone else with comparable skills must be transferred into that person's position with little or no notice. The main concern in developing this matrix is how to arrive at an understanding of the actual knowledge levels of employees in each identified area in the matrix.

- *Internal communications.* The department is well-placed to be the main provider of information to employees. The human resources staff can collect information about current conditions and the status of recovery efforts, and disseminate it to employees by a number of avenues, such as in-person meetings, text messages, and social media sites.

- *Local area communications.* In cases where a disaster impacts the immediate neighborhood (such as a release of toxic gas), the department can inform the local area of the nature of the crisis and provide information about what they should do (such as leaving the area in the short-term). These communications can mitigate the effects of lawsuits and build goodwill within the local community.

- *Memorial services.* If employees have died, then the human resources staff will be called upon to organize memorials for them.

- *Pay policy.* The department should devise a policy for how (or whether) employees are to be paid when operations are shut down due to a disaster. This policy should also address how the company will pay employees who are working extended hours to recover from a disaster.

- *Stress counseling.* Employees may have seen or experienced a workplace injury or death during a disaster, or simply been in the middle of a crisis. This can trigger a variety of stress responses, such as anxiety, an inability to concentrate, and difficulty in sleeping. The human resources staff should be on the lookout for these symptoms, and direct employees to an outside counselor who can provide confidential advice. This means that the company should subscribe to a mental health counseling program, and preferably one that provides onsite counseling.

- *Stress management techniques.* The human resources staff can include a variety of stress management training sessions, even in the absence of any disasters. Doing so shows employees what to do when their stress levels increase.
- *Substitute employees.* When employees are too overcome to continue under crisis conditions, the human resources staff can work on identifying short-term replacements for them who can fill in until these employees have recovered enough to return to work.

Information

A company may go out of business if it cannot access essential business information, perhaps because it was encrypted by a hacker under a ransomware scheme. Or, it will be at a competitive disadvantage if the information is stolen and then accessed by competitors. Alternatively, hackers may steal the information and plaster it over the Internet, damaging relations with its customers and suppliers. In all three cases, the problem is caused by criminal actions, where someone is actively trying to access company information.

There are many information best practices, all relating to security issues. In the following bullet points, we touch upon several actions that can enhance a firm's information security. However, no single item will provide comprehensive security – instead, a multi-layered approach is needed to minimize the risk of intruder access to one's information. The best practices are:

- *Data backup.* Identify any digital information that needs to be backed up, create a backup strategy for it with the most appropriate backup method, and ensure that the data backups are occurring on schedule. Several backup options are as follows:
  - *Tape backup.* Use a tape cartridge for backups. It is inexpensive and easy to store, but backups and restorations can take a long time.
  - *Cloud backup.* Use software to automatically and continuously store data in a distant server farm operated by a third party. This option works well as long as there is an Internet connection.
  - *Disk mirroring.* Copy data to two disks at the same time, so there is always an identical copy. This is especially effective when the backup disk is in a different location, so that a local disaster will not damage the backup.
  - *RAID.* Use a redundant array of disks, which are seen as a single device by the operating system. Spreading data across multiple disks increases the reliability of the data.

- *Data encryption.* Any digital information taken off-site should be encrypted. Doing so makes the information unusable for whoever steals it.
- *Default passwords.* Change the default passwords on all computer equipment as soon as it is installed. Otherwise, a hacker with knowledge of a default password can gain immediate access to key computer equipment.

- *Document shredding.* All documents tagged for destruction should be shredded, so that no one searching through the trash can glean any useful information from what they find.
- *Employee training.* Educate employees about why it is not acceptable to download files from unknown sources, since there is an increased probability that these files contain malware that can adversely impact company information.
- *Equipment destruction.* When computer equipment is obsolete, its data storage devices should be removed and destroyed, so that no one can access the information.
- *Intrusion detection systems.* Install software that monitors network traffic and flags unusual activity; this can be an early warning that hackers have penetrated the system.
- *IT access controls.* Shut down employee access to computer systems as soon as they leave the company.
- *Multifactor authentication.* Set up system access so that users are required to provide two forms of identification, such as a password and a random code that is sent to their phone.
- *Password management.* Computer software should be configured to mandate a minimum password length and complexity level, making it more difficult for hackers to guess passwords. Password management can also state the interval after which passwords must be changed, such as once a quarter or year.
- *Patching policy.* A policy should state that all patches provided by software suppliers be installed within a few days of the supplier notification. Doing so eliminates any software holes that the patches are intended to plug. This is critical, since hackers will be aggressive in exploiting vulnerabilities right away, knowing that the more capable firms will install patches as soon as possible.
- *Physical access.* The company should install enough security features around its computer systems to make it difficult for anyone to steal or access the systems. This may include access to the building, the IT work areas, and/or the data center.
- *Spam filters.* Install a spam filter to sort out any questionable inbound data traffic to the company, so that items from dubious sources can be flagged.
- *Vulnerability audits.* Hire an IT audit firm to review the company's systems and practices relating to information, and deliver a report containing recommendations for improvements.

Safety

Disasters that result in environmental damage or employee injuries can turn out to be exceedingly expensive, both directly and indirectly. A company might be subject to lawsuits resulting from the release of toxic chemicals into the local neighborhoods, or have to pay significant sums to the families of deceased employees. More indirectly, these same issues can trigger a long-lasting loss of reputation that could have an even more severe impact on a company's ability to do business. Consequently, it is essential for management to pay close attention to safety issues.

The basic approach to evaluating safety issues within an organization is to identify hazards and then assess the potential of occurrence and the severity of the associated hazard. The hazard identification process involves many areas, including the labeling of pipes, storage tanks, electrical disconnects, fall hazards, confined spaces, and dangerous machinery. Of particular interest is the development of chemical maps that note where chemicals are stored and used, as well as the presence of drains and the direction of flow for those drains.

Issues that score highly for the potential and severity of occurrence are targeted for immediate measures to mitigate the probability and severity of their occurrence. The following general actions can be taken to address identified risks:

1. Eradicate the hazard;
2. Install controls to lessen or contain the hazard (such as the use of containment dikes);
3. Install procedures to lessen or contain the hazard; and then
4. Provide personal protective equipment to employees who are exposed to the residual hazard.

When a business stores chemicals, no matter how small the quantity, it should create an inventory of what it has, where these items are located, and who uses them. In addition, the required remediation actions to take should be prominently displayed next to the chemicals in case there is a chemical spill. This documentation is usually in the form of a Material Safety Data Sheet (MSDS), which is a safety document mandated by the Occupational Safety and Health Administration. An MSDS contains information about the physical properties of a hazardous substance. A separate MSDS must be created for a number of hazardous materials, including poisonous or infectious material, compressed gases, oxidizing materials, flammable and combustible materials, and corrosive materials. Each MSDS is designed to convey chemical safety and hazard information to the end user, which includes the employees who store chemicals, employees exposed to them, and emergency responders, such as emergency medical technicians and firefighters.

An MSDS is a multi-part document that states the toxicity, use, storage, handling, and emergency procedures for hazardous substances. This means that the following categories must be included on every MSDS:

Section 1: Manufacturer's Name and Contact Information
Section 2: Hazardous Ingredients | Identity Information
Section 3: Physical | Chemical Characteristics
Section 4: Fire and Explosion Hazard Data
Section 5: Reactivity Data
Section 6: Health Hazard Data
Section 7: Precautions for Safe Handling and Use
Section 8. Control Measures

> **Tip:** The best control over chemicals is not to have the chemicals, so periodically review what is being stored to see if any can be eliminated. Alternatively, consider swapping out existing chemicals for less dangerous ones, or reducing the amount kept on-site.

> **Tip:** Maintain a list of government agencies that must be notified when there is a toxic chemical release, and post it where it will be easily accessible.

A business must also be concerned about the possibility of safety issues arising from outside the facility. For example, a nearby truck crash or train derailment can be a major issue when it is carrying toxic chemicals. This means that any adjacent railroad track or highway can be a concern, especially when it is upwind from the facility. Other safety issues coming from outside the facility include wildfires and floodwaters (which can bring in contaminants from elsewhere), as well as a breakdown in the city's water treatment facilities. Any of these outside events can trigger an immediate evacuation of the company, so a plan should be in place to shut down operations and move everyone out as expeditiously as possible.

> **Tip:** Invite the fire department for a tour of the premises at least once a year. They can provide advice about any safety enhancements to enact.

Management needs to plan for the types, quantities, and storage locations of personal protective equipment (PPE). Some of this equipment has a limited shelf life, so have a procedure to check the "use by" dates on PPE and replace it as necessary. In addition, be willing to overstock PPE, since it tends to be used up with great rapidity once a disaster occurs.

Plans to evacuate a facility are driven by local fire codes. These codes mandate the number and placement of exits, as well as the signage for those exits. Fire codes usually mandate that battery-powered or glow-in-the-dark signage be used next to exits.

Another safety concern is workplace violence. Management should develop a list of the most likely entry points to each of its facilities for an assailant, as well as where this person is most likely to go. One can then identify where security measures need to be installed to head off an inbound assailant (such as physical barriers and identification procedures), while also developing procedures to warn employees and evacuate them from targeted areas as rapidly as possible.

Once employees have been evacuated, a final step is to take a headcount to ensure that everyone has been accounted for. This can be difficult, since some employees may be off-site. Nonetheless, employees need to understand that they should remain nearby until a complete headcount has been taken and confirmed; only then can they go home. Otherwise, rescuers may spend hours searching for someone who is not on the premises.

Telecommunications

A business may have one network to handle its voice communications, which uses the standard telephone system, and a separate system for its computer network that is linked to the Internet. Others combine the two by using the Voice Over Internet Protocol (VOIP) to transmit audio communications over the Internet. Both of these networks are subject to the same types of issues, which can be addressed through proper disaster recovery planning.

The amount of funding and planning to allocate to a telephone system depends on the extent to which a company relies on it. If the firm is a call center, then it will be nonoperational whenever the phone system is not functioning. Conversely, if the business is a strawberry farm, it probably does not require much access to keep its operations humming.

The typical telephone network is designed to handle the call traffic from a relatively small proportion of the phones located within its geographic region. Whenever there is a disaster, it is a good bet that call volumes will soar – in which case the system will not be able to handle the total call volume. In this situation, a business that relies on its phones will have quite a difficult time dealing with its customers.

Before addressing ways to deal with a telecommunications disaster, we will describe the key elements of a telephone system. A telephone that uses a landline is connected through a wall jack, for which the wire is routed from a wiring closet. A wiring closet is a small room within a building where electrical connections are made. Within the wiring closet, phone wires run to a punch-down block, where the wires are punched down into short open-ended slots, which contain two metal blades that cut through the wire's insulation as it is punched down. These blades hold the wire in position and make an electrical contact with the wire. Wires run from the wiring closet to a firm's telephone switching equipment, which is commonly referred to as a private branch exchange (PBX). A PBX automates the task of connecting calls to specific phones. If a call is intended for a telephone number external to the business, then the PBX connects the call to the local phone company's central office via a trunk line, from which the call is shunted to the receiving phone. A trunk line is a direct line between two telephone switchboards. Other equipment is likely to be positioned alongside the PBX, including an interactive voice response system (used to manage an automated phone menu), a port selector (to connect inbound calls to the first available employee), and a call monitoring system (which tracks the level of call activity).

A computer network within a business is most commonly configured with a set of servers that store data and programs held in common across the organization. Users can access these data either through wired or wireless connections, where the connections are handled by switches that manage the flow of traffic between the servers and user workstations. In addition, routers are used to move packets of data between workstations and the Internet. Internet connections are usually through a single line to an Internet service provider (ISP). Routers and switches are positioned in a network closet.

When devising a plan to deal with telecommunications issues, review the business impact analysis for this area (as described in an earlier chapter). The analysis will likely deal with such issues as cut cables, water damage to electronics, and hacker attacks. The points highlighted in the analysis can then be used to enact a set of best practices that apply to the mitigation and prevention of disasters relating to telecommunications. The following are examples of such best practices:

- *Access restrictions*. Wiring closets and network closets should be considered critical to company operations – which means restricting access to authorized employees.
- *Air circulation*. The equipment in a network closet creates heat, so ensure that there are enough vents and fans in the closet to maintain relatively low temperatures within it.
- *Closet clearing*. There should be nothing in a wiring closet or network closet other than the equipment – which means no flammable materials that can trigger a fire. These closets are not storage areas for random supplies.
- *Closet inspections*. Review all wiring closets and network closets to see if water pipes run over them. If so, set up a periodic inspection schedule to see if there are developing cracks that could result in water leaks.
- *Closet lighting*. The lighting in a wiring closet and network closet should be quite good, since technicians trying to conduct repairs will need to engage in quite detailed work in these areas.
- *Do not dig warnings*. When cables run underground from the building, mark them with "do not dig" warning signs, so that a backhoe operator does not cut through them.
- *Fire suppression*. Wiring closets and network closets may not have any staff nearby, so install fire alarm and fire suppression systems in them.
- *ISP guarantees*. When there is a choice of ISP, pick the one with the highest guaranteed system availability time.
- *ISP links*. A major weakness in many companies is the single line going to a firm's ISP. If Internet access is essential to the business, then acquire a second line that goes to a second ISP. Make sure that the two cables are separate, so that an event cutting one line will not also cut the other line. This can be a problem in low-traffic areas, where two ISPs might normally arrange to share the same line.
- *Landline usage*. It can be useful to maintain at least one landline going into a facility, because this line may still work even when there is a power failure (which may also terminate power to the local cell phone tower). The landline can then be used to call the power company to notify them of the power failure.
- *Network monitoring software*. Install network monitoring software, which automatically reviews network traffic and issues warnings when equipment is about to fail, so that recovery can be initiated more quickly.
- *PBX backups*. As may be apparent from the discussion thus far, a PBX (and all associated equipment) is a prime point of failure. Thus, one should prepare for it by making backup copies of the configuration data for each device in the PBX cluster, and store some of the backups off-site.

- *Power backup.* If telephone or data traffic is considered essential to company operations, then install a robust UPS to continue providing power to it in the event of a power failure.
- *Privately-owned devices policy.* Institute a policy that no privately-owned devices can be used to access the company network. Doing so reduces the risk that computer viruses on these devices will find their way into the company network.
- *Redundant communications.* If the telephone system fails, have radios, cell phones, and possibly even satellite phones on hand in order to engage in the more critical communications.
- *Redundant devices.* Consider installing an extra router, switch, and so forth, so that service can be transferred over if the primary device fails.
- *Standardize.* Try to acquire the same type of computer hardware and software, so that spares can be kept on hand and more easily integrated into the system if the originals fail. The configurations for these items should also be standardized, for the same reason.
- *Wireless backup.* If the main in-house network runs over cables and they fail, a possible backup option is to have a wireless system available and ready to go – though it will need to be configured with encryption to maintain the security of company data.
- *Wiring inventory.* Create a map of all cable runs within the facility, as well as where cables enter the building. This information is needed to restore service when wires are damaged.

When an organization has converted to VOIP, audio calls are transmitted through a workstation's data connection to the Internet. This approach eliminates the need for a separate telephone network, but suffers from having both audio and data running through one data connection.

> **Note:** Most phone lines are digital, in order to accommodate the most recent PBX systems. However, a company may still have a few analog lines, which are used for alarm systems and the occasional modem connection. These lines will have to be tracked and maintained separately.

Terrorism

Terrorism, according to the federal government, is "the unlawful use of force and violence against persons or property to intimidate or coerce a government, the civilian population, or any segment thereof, in furtherance of political or social objectives." Any business may be the subject of a terrorist attack, if doing so provides sufficient publicity to further the cause of a terrorist organization. For example, a United States corporation that operates a subsidiary in a terrorist-prone country is at increased risk of a terrorist attack, because it is a symbol of the "decadent" west. Or, any sort of controversial business or military supplier could be at increased risk of an attack. The focus of an attack might even be as minor as having a controversial member of the government as a minority shareholder. In these cases, the main role of management is to harden the business against terrorist attack, so that it is an unappealing target. The level of hardening will need to be increased if the location appears to be of higher value to a terrorist. For example, a terrorist might be more inclined to attack a landmark building whose destruction has some sort of symbolic significance, or a government building; if the company is located adjacent to or within one of these structures, it may be at higher risk of an attack. Possible facility hardening options are:

- Block adjacent parking, so that bomb-laden vehicles will have to park further away, thereby reducing the impact of the blast.
- Ensure that all doors are locked and guarded.
- Build a concrete wall between the company facility and the potential target, to minimize blast damage.
- Place concrete obstacles around the facility to keep vehicles from driving into it.
- Install crash gates, which are raised barriers used to prevent vehicles from entering a restricted area.
- Remove trash cans from around the facility, since bombs can be hidden inside them.
- Install heavy curtains with weighted bottoms to cover windows. Doing so blocks inbound flying glass from any explosions outside.
- Install bulletproof glass, to prevent bullets or other projectiles from entering.
- Confine freight pickups and deliveries to a few hours per day, when they can be closely inspected.
- Locate IT equipment in the farthest corner of the facility from the potential target, so the rest of the facility will cushion the equipment from a blast.
- Move the most sensitive operations to a more innocuous location, or move all company operations elsewhere.

In addition, a company may need to provide training and/or protection to key employees, if there is a concern that they may be killed or kidnapped by terrorists. These individuals are especially prone to violence, since they probably live away from the protection of the company's facilities. Actions they can take to reduce this risk include taking different routes to and from work each day, and keeping their travel itineraries as vague as possible. Other actions that they can be advised to take include the following:

- *Avoid packages.* An unattended package can be a bomb, so keep any such items at a considerable distance.
- *Hire security.* When traveling in a questionable area, hire security for protection, as well as a driver who knows the area.
- *Look unimportant.* Do everything possible to blend in, including wearing nondescript clothing.
- *Sidestep crowds.* Terrorists like to attack crowds in order to cause maximum damage, so stay away from large gatherings.

- *Spot exits.* Always be aware of the avenues of escape from a public place, in case an attack occurs.

In short, when there is any hint of a risk of terrorist activity, take appropriate steps to harden company facilities and protect employees. Even though the risk may be low, the amount of damage and injuries that may be incurred is quite high.

Summary

Some types of business records are absolutely essential to the continued operation of a business, and so require extensive preventive measures to minimize any damage to them. In addition, employees should be trained in how to deal with damaged records, so that they are handled correctly to minimize damage during the recovery process.

The key lesson in regard to computer workstations is that, over time, they *will* fail. To mitigate the fallout from these failures, be sure to impose a backup policy for critical files, while also controlling the use of software and ensuring that computers are replaced at regular intervals.

Constructing a proper system of surge protectors, power conditioners, UPS units and power generators – properly maintained – is an essential guard against the effects of a disaster, since most organizations cannot operate at all without a supply of electricity. Similarly, one should thoroughly protect a firm's system of telecommunications, including setting up a system of redundant communications in case the primary systems fail.

Safety is a major concern. Management should have reviewed all company facilities to spot potential hazards, mitigated them where possible, and installed controls to deal with any remaining issues. These tasks are essential for minimizing employee injuries, as well as any impacts on the surrounding community. Doing so protects the financial health of the business, as well as its reputation.

The human resources department can provide invaluable service during a crisis. It can work with employees to make their individual situations easier, while also arranging for counseling to mitigate the worst emotional effects of the event. Another valuable role is to adjust work policies to match the realities of the situation.

When dealing with customers and suppliers, the key point relating to disasters is communications. Tell them when there is a problem, and how it will impact their operations. Being seen as open and trustworthy is a key aspect of being a long-term business partner for them.

A final planning concern is acts of terrorism. Management should analyze the susceptibility of company operations to attack. Based on this review, it may be necessary to harden certain facilities to minimize the damage from a prospective attack, as well as to advise employees on how to minimize their risks related to terrorist actions.

Glossary

B

Business impact analysis. The process of determining the criticality of business activities to ensure that operations remain resilient both during and after a business disruption.

D

Disaster. A sudden, calamitous event that seriously disrupts the functioning of a business.

Disaster recovery. The process of resuming normal operations following a disaster by finding alternative work locations, restoring communications, and regaining access to company data and connectivity.

M

Material safety data sheet. A safety document mandated by the Occupational Safety and Health Administration for the storage and handling of certain materials.

P

Pandemic. An epidemic of an infectious disease that has spread across a large region.

R

Recovery point objective. The amount of data that can be lost before a company function is seriously compromised.

Recovery time objective. The amount of time that a specific function can be nonoperational before the entity suffers from it.

Risk. The probability of a negative outcome.

Risk analysis. The process of identifying potential threats to an organization.

W

Work breakdown structure. A key project deliverable that organizes a team's work into manageable sections.

Index

www.ingramcontent.com/pod-product-compliance
Lightning Source LLC
Chambersburg PA
CBHW051351200326
41521CB00014B/2533